Love *(handwritten inscription)*

Spiritual VITAMINS

DR. JOHN E. GUNS

ISBN: 1537611550
ISBN-13: 978-1537611556

Dedication

To my amazing wife, Sonjanique, our beautiful daughters, Alexis, Daijah, and Tayler, and yes, to my grandson, Zion, know I love you so much and you are forever in my heart.

To my parents, Dr. Frank and Rev. Quincey Guns, thank you for teaching me to love your God. I am who I am because of you.

And finally to my St. Paul Church of Jacksonville family, thank you for your love, encouragement, inspiration, and commitment to capturing many great moments of the ministry that God has given me. For over 20 years we have walked together and I am forever indebted to you. What an extraordinary church!

For all who will read *Spiritual Vitamins,* know it is not only a book filled with incredible, God-given thoughts, but it's a part of a legacy that's designed to impact generations of believers. Enjoy the journey. And seize the moment!

Contents

About Dr. John E. Guns

John E. Guns is the Senior Pastor of St. Paul Church of Jacksonville, Inc. where he has totally revived what was once a rigid, placid, traditional southern Baptist church into an oasis of FAITH, FELLOWSHIP and FUN. Through extremely innovative thinking and an approachable spirit, Dr. Guns has epitomized koinonia before this great congregation and has ultimately built an amazing community of worshipers. His love for worship is evident whenever the St. Paul family gathers! He was formally educated in the public and private school system of Hampton Roads, VA.

He earned his Bachelor's of Art degree in Sociology from Norfolk State University and his Masters of Divinity and Doctoral of Ministry Degrees from the Samuel Dewitt Proctor School of Theology, Virginia Union University.

Because of his passion for worship and education, Bishop Guns is the Dean of Gospel Heritage Praise & Worship Conference and is Co-Founder/Managing Partner of The Cloud Music, LLC, which declares the message of Jesus Christ through an innovative and transforming sound. Their first musical project, "I See The Cloud", released June 2013 promises to liberate and transform the lives of many by showcasing an amazing diversity of sounds and gifts.

In November of 2014, Dr. Guns was asked by His Grace, Bishop Neil C. Ellis, to serve as the leader of Christian Education of Global United Fellowship. As a result of this appointment, he was consecrated to the office of Bishop on July 18, 2014.

Bishop Guns is the Founder of Operation Save Our Sons, a national movement to work with At-Risk boys designed to equip them to make positive decisions regarding the law & authority. He works on several boards and community based organizations. Bishop Guns is an active member of Kappa Alpha Psi Inc. Of all his accomplishments, his most important is his family. Bishop Guns is the proud husband and life partner of Lady Sonjanique L. Guns and loving father of three daughters, Alexis, Daijah, and Tayler.

Vitamin A

APPLYING THE WORD OF GOD

Applying the Word of God

It is evident and obvious that if anyone desires to successfully navigate the journey of discipleship, they must be willing to engage in a disciplined study of the Word of God. It is virtually impossible to live a faithful, focused life and not submit daily to what God declares in his word. The value of this time of study leads to consistent application of the Word of God. We call this OBEDIENCE. Obedience becomes the measurement of your faith and in turn it determines your ability to live a life that honors God.

Vitamin A is designed to enhance your spiritual growth by inspiring you the reader to not only consistently read the Word of God, but to take the time to apply it to your life on a daily basis. The intense application of the Word of God is paramount to your personal success. The person who chooses to live out faith daily through application or OBEDIENCE will find themselves wonderfully empowered to face the challenges of life. In turn, whether these challenges are expected or unexpected, the potency of the Word of God will cause you to forge forward, fulfilling the plans that God (according to Jeremiah 29:11) has for you.

The application of the Word of God thus no longer changes your way of thinking but ultimately changes your way of existing. The importance of Vitamin A is that as you digest it spiritually and intellectually each day. You will find yourself moved to OBEY and inspired to MODEL. You will be awakened to the fact that nothing is impossible and you will desire more of God. Each vitamin will speak deeply to you and you will seek God with greater fervency.

Day 1

"DISCIPLINE YOUR ISSUES SO THEY DON'T INTERFERE WITH YOUR PRODUCTIVITY."

Points to Ponder

In what way(s) do you lack discipline? What issues can you eliminate in order to become more productive?

_____

_____

_____

_____

_____

_____

Day 2

"WHATEVER YOU SAY OUT YOUR MOUTH IS THE RECORD OF YOUR LIFE."

Points to Ponder

Write down at least three of your current expectations and declare them daily.

_____

_____

_____

_____

_____

_____

Day 3

"OBEDIENCE CAN'T BE VIEWED BY BLIND PEOPLE."

Points to Ponder

How can you demonstrate a greater level of obedience within your relationship with God?

_____

_____

_____

_____

_____

_____

Day 4

"SOME PEOPLE IN YOUR LIFE
COME WITH EXPIRATION DATES
BUT YOU'VE TRIED TO MAKE
THEM NON-PERISHABLE.
KNOW WHEN THE SEASON IS
UP!"

Points to Ponder

Examine your current relationships. Do they
align with the plans God has for you?

_____

_____

_____

_____

_____

_____

Day 5

"A GODLY WOMAN IS
SUBMISSIVE AND HUMBLE IN
ALL SITUATIONS—NOT JUST
CERTAIN CIRCUMSTANCES."

Points to Ponder

Are traits of submission and humility a part of
your personality?

_____

_____

_____

_____

_____

_____

Day 6

"MAKE SURE PAST MISTAKES
DON'T GET PRESENT SPACE.
BECOME HEALTHIER, HOLIER
AND HAPPIER EACH DAY."

Read Psalms 51.

Points to Ponder

Write down at least 3 keys that will assist you in becoming healthier, holier, and happier.

_____

_____

_____

_____

_____

_____

Day 7

"STOP LETTING THE ENEMY
BAIT YOU INTO MOMENTS THAT
WEAKEN YOUR FAITH AND
CAUSE YOU TO DECLARE
DEFEAT BEFORE THE BATTLE."

Points to Ponder

Read Hebrews 11 and write down some of the areas in which you need God to strengthen your faith.

_____

_____

_____

_____

_____

_____

Day 8

"GIFT PLUS ARROGANCE IS THE RECIPE FOR DESTRUCTION. DEVELOP HUMILITY AND YOU WILL LIVE."

Points to Ponder

Write down the areas in which God has gifted you, and make a declaration that He will allow you to remain humble so that He can receive the glory from your labor.

_____

_____

_____

_____

_____

_____

Day 9

"DISCONNECTING EGO FROM ASSIGNMENT WILL ENSURE YOU AREN'T TRYING TO KEEP UP WITH SOMEONE ELSE'S PACE. TRUST WHERE GOD HAS YOU AND VALUE YOUR ASSIGNMENT."

Points to Ponder

Take the time today to write out the assignment God has given you.

_____

_____

_____

_____

_____

_____

Day 10

"NEVER THINK THAT YOU HAVE ARRIVED WHEN HE IS STILL BUILDING ROADS!"

Read Philippians 3:14.

Points to Ponder

Make a commitment to growing in Christ daily. Write down the areas that you desire for Him to develop within you.

_____

_____

_____

_____

_____

_____

Day 11

"DON'T GET STUCK WHERE HE WANTS YOU TO BEGIN!"

Read Genesis 19:26.

Points to Ponder

Ask God to give you the desire to make progress. List the goals you want to achieve.

_____

_____

_____

_____

_____

_____

Day 12

"YOU DIDN'T SEE WHAT WAS COMING BECAUSE YOU GOT STUCK IN WHAT WAS!"

Points to Ponder

Be determined not to dwell on the past. What are some of the things that have hindered you from completely moving forward?

_____

_____

_____

_____

_____

_____

Day 13

"BECOME AN ARSONIST OF YOUR PRESENT PAST."

Read 1 Kings 19:19-21.

Points to Ponder

Read I Kings 19:19-21 and write down your thoughts.

_____

_____

_____

_____

_____

_____

Day 14

"YOU FIRED YOURSELF WITH YOUR FAITH!"

Points to Ponder

Commit to allowing God to lead you. Read Proverbs 3:5-6. How can you submit more to God's leading?

_____

_____

_____

_____

_____

_____

Day 15

"CRAVE GOD AND WATCH GOD SATISFY YOU!"

Points to Ponder

Read Matthew 5:6 and record your thoughts concerning what it means to be "hungry" for God.

_____

_____

_____

_____

_____

_____

Day 16

"SIMPLICITY AND SINGLENESS OF HEART ARE THE ALLIES TO REST! GOD RELEASES REST TODAY!"

Points to Ponder

What can you do to simplify your life so that you can rest in the presence of God?

_____

_____

_____

_____

_____

_____

Day 17

"TODAY WE **REST!** **REST** IS
CONFIDENTLY KNOWING THAT
GOD IS IN CONTROL. AS YOU
OBEY, GOD IS WORKING ON
YOUR BEHALF."

Read Isaiah 26:3 & Philippians 4:6.

Points to Ponder

After reading Isaiah 26:3 and Philippians 4:6,
reflect on why it's so important to rest in God
and obey His word.

_____

_____

_____

_____

_____

_____

Day 18

"THE ENEMY'S JOB IS TO CONTAMINATE YOUR THINKING, TWISTING YOUR PERCEPTION OF THE PROCESS THAT'S ORDAINED FOR YOU TO BECOME GREAT."

Points to Ponder

Today, make a commitment to the unique process that God has for you. List those things that may be hindering or distracting you.

_____

_____

_____

_____

_____

_____

Day 19

"DON'T DESIRE TO BE WITH
SOMEONE WHO IS
COMFORTABLE WATCHING YOU
LAY IN THE VOMIT OF YOUR
DYSFUNCTION."

Points to Ponder

Evaluate each of your current relationships.
Does each of them provide support and
encouragement? Which ones should be
eliminated?

_____

_____

_____

_____

_____

_____

Day 20

"STUART SCOTT WAS BELOVED
BECAUSE HE ENCOURAGED
EVERYBODY AROUND HIM.
HE SENT TEXTS, LEFT
VOICEMAILS AND WROTE
PERSONAL NOTES OF
ENCOURAGEMENT."

Points to Ponder

How can you be a better encourager to the
people God places in your path? Read the story
of Barnabus in Acts 4.

Day 21

"IT'S TRUE THAT WHEN YOU
ARE NICE TO PEOPLE, YOU
WILL BE MISSED. TREAT
OTHERS KINDLY AND WATCH
GOD HONOR YOU."

Points to Ponder

Strive to treat the people you come into contact with kindly. List the names of people you can impact positively through kind treatment.

_____

_____

_____

_____

_____

_____

Day 22

"HUMILITY IS THE KEY TO PROMOTION."

Points to Ponder

Read James 4:10 and list some of the ways in which you can demonstrate a greater level of humility, so that God can promote you later.

_____

_____

_____

_____

_____

_____

Day 23

"IN THE *BOOK OF ELI*, ELI
(DENZEL) SAID, 'I'VE BEEN SO
BUSY KEEPING THE BOOK SAFE I
FORGOT TO LIVE BY WHAT I
LEARNED FROM IT.' WHAT A
REMINDER! THE WORD MUST BE
LIVED—NOT JUST DISCUSSED AND
PROTECTED!"

Points to Ponder

What changes can you make right now to
ensure that you are living out God's word to
the very best of your ability?

_____

_____

_____

_____

_____

_____

Day 24

"BE CAREFUL HOW YOU HANDLE THOSE GOD USES TO GET YOU BACK ON YOUR FEET! NEVER OUTGROW BEING GRATEFUL!"

Points to Ponder

List the names of everyone God has used to assist you during tough times. Say a special prayer for them.

_____

_____

_____

_____

_____

_____

Day 25

"DON'T ABORT YOUR DREAMS
BECAUSE OF A MISTAKE OR
FAILURE. I'M AN EXAMPLE
THAT SECOND CHANCES EXIST.
GOD CAN ENABLE YOU TO DO
IT AGAIN!"

Points to Ponder

No matter what you experience, God can give
you a second chance. Write down the areas of
your life in which you need Him to do it.

_____

_____

_____

_____

_____

_____

Day 26

"FOLLOW YOUR BOTHERED TO THE BETTER."

Points to Ponder

What's bothering you right now? How can you take what is bothering you and allow it to make you better?

_____

_____

_____

_____

_____

_____

Day 27

"DON'T THINK THAT THE FACT
GOD ALLOWS YOU TO SERVE IS
A STATEMENT THAT GOD IS
PLEASED. COME DAILY
BEFORE GOD IN PRAYER,
CONFESSING YOUR NEED FOR
GOD!"

Points to Ponder

Write a commitment on how you can be
pleasing God in every area of your life.

_____

_____

_____

_____

_____

_____

Day 28

"WHEN I WORK OUT I LISTEN TO
AUDIOBOOKS. THAT TIME IS NOT
ONLY IMPACTING MY HEALTH BUT
MY MIND. CREATE A LIFE OF
BALANCE. IT'S TAKEN ME YEARS
BUT I'M BETTER AT IT NOW
BECAUSE I'M PUTTING FORTH THE
EFFORT."

Points to Ponder

List the ways that you can create more balance
in your life spiritually, emotionally, personally,
and professionally.

_____

_____

_____

_____

_____

_____

Day 29

"STOP COMPLAINING, START PRODUCING."

Points to Ponder

Write down three short term goals and three long term goals. Make a commitment to getting them done and create a plan to do so.

_____

_____

_____

_____

_____

_____

Day 30

"DON'T LOSE SLEEP OVER PEOPLE WHO ARE NOT ORDAINED TO BE THERE AT THE END!"

Points to Ponder

Identify ways to release the burden of other people so that you maintain a healthy relationship while removing the stress.

_____

_____

_____

_____

_____

_____

Day 31

"NEVER OVERESTIMATE THE
STRENGTH OF YOUR ENEMIES
WHEN THE STRENGTH AND
SOURCE OF YOUR LIFE IS GOD. IN
THE END, GOD CONTROLS THEM
AND WILL EQUIP YOU TO FORGIVE
THEM FOR THE SAKE OF GREATER
GLORY."

Read Psalms 110:1.

Points to Ponder

Read Psalm 110:1 and write down your thoughts of reflection.

_____

_____

_____

_____

_____

_____

Day 32

"THREE SIMPLE WORDS: LET IT GO!"

Points to Ponder

Today, cast ALL of your cares on the Lord! Read Psalm 55:22 and write at least three things you're releasing to God.

_____

_____

_____

_____

_____

_____

Day 33

"IT IS CLEAR THAT GOD HAS TRUSTED YOU WITH A NEW DAY! THE QUESTION IS: WHAT WILL YOU DO WITH IT? HOW WILL YOU APPROACH THE UNPLANNED EVENTS WITHIN IT? HOW WILL YOU HANDLE THE UNSCRIPTED MOMENTS? MY SUGGESTION IS TO BE GRATEFUL AND ENJOY!"

Read Psalms 118:24.

Points to Ponder

Read Psalm 118:24 and summarize it in your own words.

_____

_____

_____

_____

_____

_____

Day 34

"ALLOW LIFE TO BE A TUTOR—NOT A JUDGE."

Points to Ponder

Write down some of the experiences you have had in life and the lesson that you learned from them.

_____

_____

_____

_____

_____

_____

Day 35

"DON'T ABORT UNITY JUST TO GET YOUR WAY."

Points to Ponder

Take the time to think about various associations that you can impact through the power of unity. These associations may include your family, co-workers, classmates, ministry groups, etc.

_____

_____

_____

_____

_____

_____

Day 36

"IT'S NOT ABOUT HOW PEOPLE
MANAGE YOU, BUT IT'S ALL
ABOUT HOW YOU MANAGE
PEOPLE."

Points to Ponder

Write down the name of one person who is
currently mismanaging you. Write down what
you can do to ensure that you DO NOT
mismanage them.

_____

_____

_____

_____

_____

_____

Day 37

"OBSCURITY ISN'T YOUR PROBLEM—YOUR PROBLEM IS YOUR IMPATIENCE WITH THE QUIET."

Points to Ponder

List some of the challenges that come with being impatient and how these challenges may affect you. Make a vow to God to demonstrate more patience.

_____

_____

_____

_____

_____

_____

Day 38

"YOU MUST CONQUER YOUR OWN THOUGHTS BEFORE YOU CAN CONQUER THE OPINIONS OF OTHERS."

Points to Ponder

What negative thoughts do you need to conquer in order to make progress in life?

_____

_____

_____

_____

_____

_____

Day 39

"YOU HELPED ME WHEN YOU HURT ME."

Points to Ponder

How can you take the painful experiences you have had in life and use them to help you become a better person?

_____

_____

_____

_____

_____

_____

Day 40

"YOU HAVE TO BE AN IDIOT TO THROW UP THE MEDICINE."

Points to Ponder

Make a commitment to receiving healthy counsel, advice, wisdom, or any other spiritual "medicine" that is designed to help you.

_____

_____

_____

_____

_____

_____

Day 41

"IT'S IMPOSSIBLE TO DO VISION WITH VISION-LESS PEOPLE."

Points to Ponder

Read Proverbs 29:18 and make a healthy commitment to partnering with the vision that God has assigned you to—especially in your local church. Write down the vision of that organization, and also begin to write the vision for your own life.

_____

_____

_____

_____

_____

_____

Day 42

"DISCIPLINE YOUR CONFESSIONS!"

Points to Ponder

Make positive confessions a part of your daily routine. Make a list of positive things you are expecting God to do in your life and in the lives of those connected to you.

_____

_____

_____

_____

_____

_____

Day 43

"WHEN PEOPLE POORLY
MANAGE INSECURITIES, THEY
CREATE A WORLD OF NEGATIVE
THOUGHTS."

Points to Ponder

What are some of your insecurities? What triggers them? How can you manage them better?

_____

_____

_____

_____

_____

_____

Day 44

"WHEN INSECURITIES ARE
NOT MANAGED WELL, IT
ULTIMATELY CREATES A
LIFESTYLE OF DAMAGE."

Points to Ponder

What are you personally risking by not properly managing your insecurities (relationships, opportunities, etc.)?

_____

_____

_____

_____

_____

_____

Day 45

"WHAT GOOD IS IT TO GET CAUGHT UP IN YOUR GIFT IF YOU CONTINUE TO MISS YOUR SEASON?"

Points to Ponder

Identify time(s) in your life when you had a great opportunity but missed the season due to lack of preparedness.

_____

_____

_____

_____

_____

_____

Day 46

"WHEN YOU DO IT GOD'S WAY,
THE PROCESS MAY BE LONGER
BUT WHEN YOUR SEASON
COMES IT WILL PEACEFUL."

Points to Ponder

How can you insure that you don't rush the
process that God has given you?

_____

_____

_____

_____

_____

_____

Day 47

"WHEN YOU OBEY GOD IN ASSIGNMENT, PEOPLE CAN NEVER DUPLICATE WHAT HE DID SUPERNATURALLY!"

Points to Ponder

Strive to be obedient to God and His commandments. Read John 14:15 and write down your thoughts.

_____

_____

_____

_____

_____

_____

Day 48

"VICTORY COMES WHEN YOU
CAN PICK UP THE ENEMY
BEFORE HE PICKS YOU UP."

Points to Ponder

Spend time in prayer with God so that you can
be better prepared for what the enemy may be
plotting concerning you and your family. Write
down what God shows you, and pray that He
will intervene on your behalf.

_____

_____

_____

_____

_____

_____

Day 49

"REVIVAL SHOULDN'T HAPPEN IN THE CHURCH—IT SHOULD HAPPEN THROUGH THE CHURCH."

Points to Ponder

Write down some ways in which God can use your life to bring revival to the people around you, and amongst your family, friends, co-workers, classmates, community, etc.

_____

_____

_____

_____

_____

_____

Day 50

"DESIRE TO BE HAPPY!"

Points to Ponder

Make a declaration and commitment to God
that you WILL live happily. Write down things
that you can do personally to aid in your
happiness.

_____

_____

_____

_____

_____

_____

Day 51

"WISDOM, LOVE AND OBEDIENCE!"

Points to Ponder

How can you demonstrate a greater level of wisdom, love, and obedience in your walk with Jesus Christ?

_____

_____

_____

_____

_____

_____

Day 52

"WHEN YOU GET HURT BY PEOPLE, IT WILL PARALYZE YOU."

Points to Ponder

Who do you need to forgive so that the fact that they hurt you doesn't result in you being paralyzed?

_____

_____

_____

_____

_____

Day 53

"HEALTHY RELATIONSHIPS ARE KEY FOR PERSONAL GROWTH."

Points to Ponder

Make a strong effort to insure that you maintain healthy personal and professional relationships. What are some indicators of a healthy relationship?

_____

_____

_____

_____

_____

_____

Day 54

"DON'T ACT LIKE IT DIDN'T HAPPEN. ADMIT YOUR PAIN, HEAL, AND MOVE ON!"

Points to Ponder

Write down the experiences you've had that have caused you pain and write the declaration that God WILL heal you from them.

_____

_____

_____

_____

_____

_____

Day 55

"SOME OF YOUR WORSE PAINS CAME FROM PEOPLE— ESPECIALLY THE ONES YOU TRUSTED."

Points to Ponder

If you have been hurt by anyone close to you, make the decision to not only forgive them, but to also allow the experience to make you a better person. Write down how you will do that.

_____

_____

_____

_____

_____

_____

Day 56

"YOU HAVE TOO MANY PEOPLE IN YOUR EAR WHO DOESN'T HAVE GOD'S HEART."

Points to Ponder

Who have you given access to that does not have God's heart?

_____

_____

_____

_____

_____

_____

Day 57

"WHATEVER YOU GO THROUGH, DON'T LET IT DESTROY YOU."

Points to Ponder

What commitments or adjustments are you willing to make to ensure that what you may go through doesn't destroy you?

_____

_____

_____

_____

_____

_____

Day 58

"LEARN HOW TO END RELATIONSHIPS DURING TRANSITION."

Points to Ponder

If God takes you through a season of transition, how will you approach ending relationships?

_____

_____

_____

_____

_____

_____

Day 59

"FAVOR IN FAMINE COMES
WHEN YOU SEEK DIRECTION
FROM GOD AND NOT THE
PEOPLE IN YOUR FAMINE."

Points to Ponder

Make the commitment to seek God whenever
you go through famine. Write down your
thoughts on ways that you can insure that you
spend more time with Him and less time with
people.

_____

_____

_____

_____

_____

_____

Day 60

"EVEN WHEN YOU GO THROUGH ADVERSITY, KEEP A SONG IN YOUR HEART AND A SMILE ON YOUR FACE."

Points to Ponder

What are your favorite worship songs? Write down the ones that you will commit to singing unto God whenever you face adversity.

_____

_____

_____

_____

_____

_____

Day 61

"STOP LOOKING FOR YOUR
EXIT IN ADVERSITY. IT'S JUST A
SEASON."

Points to Ponder

Write down a strategy to help you better
endure adversity rather than looking for a way
out of it.

_____

_____

_____

_____

_____

_____

Day 62

"INSERT PEOPLE WHO MAKE YOU BETTER."

Points to Ponder

Who has God placed around you that is designed to make you better?

_____

_____

_____

_____

_____

_____

Day 63

"DO THE PEOPLE IN YOUR CIRCLE CARRY WEIGHT OR PUT WEIGHT ON YOU?"

Points to Ponder

Who is currently around you that makes your life more difficult? How will you manage your relationship with them?

_____

_____

_____

_____

_____

_____

Day 64

"STOP CHASING PEOPLE WHO ARE ONLY HERE FOR A SEASON."

Points to Ponder

Commit to more time in prayer and studying the Word of God so that your relationship with Him will become stronger than it is with people who may only be seasonal.

_____

_____

_____

_____

_____

_____

Day 65

"THE MORE YOU GROW, THE MORE YOUR CIRCLE CHANGES."

Points to Ponder

What does "growth" mean to you? Are the people around you a reflection of your growth? If not, why do you think that is?

_____

_____

_____

_____

_____

_____

Day 66

"DAVID USED HIS INFLUENCE TO EMBRACE A COMMITMENT TO FULFILL ASSIGNMENT."

Points to Ponder

What are your current areas of influence? Are you using your influence to embrace the totality of your assignment?

_____

_____

_____

_____

_____

Day 67

"CONNECT WITH PEOPLE WHO MAKE YOU BETTER."

Points to Ponder

Are the connections you make to people causing you to become better? What are you looking for in personal and professional relationships?

_____

_____

_____

_____

_____

_____

Day 68

"ELEVATION IS NOT POPULARITY."

Points to Ponder

What does elevation mean to you? Are you willing to become less popular in order to be elevated?

_____

_____

_____

_____

_____

_____

Day 69

"EVERY STAGE OF LIFE BRINGS YOU INTO A GREATER OPPORTUNITY."

Points to Ponder

What opportunities is God giving you *right now*? How will you take advantage of those opportunities?

_____

_____

_____

_____

_____

_____

Day 70

"IF YOU DON'T DEVELOP YOUR SKILLS, YOU'RE NOT READY FOR THE PRESSURE."

Points to Ponder

God has given all of us skills and gifts. Have you made a commitment to developing those skills? How can you better develop your skills and gifts?

_____

_____

_____

_____

_____

_____

Day 71

"DON'T WANT SOMETHING YOU'RE NOT WILLING TO PAY THE PRICE FOR."

Points to Ponder

Make a list of the things that you really want out of life. Are you willing to pay whatever price is necessary to achieve these things? How far are you willing to go?

_____

_____

_____

_____

_____

_____

Day 72

"THE HARDER YOUR LIFE IS, THE GREATER YOU PERFORM."

Points to Ponder

Write down some of the more difficult experiences you've had in life and how you were able to overcome them. Take those examples and strive to have the same kind of resiliency if you happen to face challenges in the future.

_____

_____

_____

_____

_____

_____

Day 73

"BE CAREFUL WHO YOU MODEL YOURSELF AFTER."

Points to Ponder

Who are you modeling yourself after? Do they possess the characteristics of Jesus Christ?

_____

_____

_____

_____

_____

_____

Day 74

"YOUR GREATEST ALLY TO
MATURITY ARE YOUR
ENEMIES."

Points to Ponder

Have you been allowing your enemies to make
you more mature? Write down your personal
keys to successfully dealing with enemies.

_____

_____

_____

_____

_____

_____

Vitamin B

BELIEVING GOD

Believing the Word of God

Paul in Romans 10:17 writes, "So then, faith comes from hearing the message, and the message comes through preaching Christ." While this verse speaks to faith as what is needed to experience salvation from and through Jesus Christ, it also provides the formula for growing your faith. Because life is sometimes so "interesting" it is important to develop a faith that is both enduring and empowering. This results from your belief system. A belief system as defined by Gerhard Adams are "the stories we tell ourselves to define our personal sense of "reality".

Every human being has a belief system that they utilize, and it is through this mechanism that we individually, "make sense" of the world around us. The value of your faith is that while a belief system is framed from it, it ultimately equips you to victoriously manage life. Your faith then is the pillar that stabilizes you. This enables you to face life's unique demands while producing with the liberating help of the Holy Spirit narrative of victories. In the end, every force designed to destroy you ends up working in your favor. This is the immeasurable value of Vitamin B.

Vitamin B is designed to enhance your spiritual growth by building and strengthening your faith through Godly thoughts of encouragement, empowerment, and inspiration. So, as you digest your daily vitamin, be prepared to see your faith explode and your life take on new meaning. This vitamin will push you to explore intimately the God who has—through the sacrifice of Jesus Christ—redeemed us. You will feel urgency without being impatient. What an amazing journey will commence and you will not allow anything to disrupt you. For you shall walk by faith and not simply what you see.

Day 75

"LET NO ONE **EVER** MAKE LIGHT OF WHAT GOD IS DOING IN YOUR LIFE."

Points to Ponder

Make a list of things that you notice God doing for you and the impact that it's having on the people around you.

_____

_____

_____

_____

_____

_____

Day 76

"ENJOY YOUR JOURNEY OF
INTIMACY WITH GOD AND
CELEBRATE YOUR GROWTH."

Points to Ponder

What are you doing daily to ensure that you
grow closer and closer to God? How will
growing closer to God impact your everyday
journey?

_____

_____

_____

_____

_____

_____

Day 77

"LET ME ENCOURAGE YOU:
STAY FAITHFUL AND
WHEREVER YOU ARE RIGHT
NOW IS WHERE GOD IS GOING
TO QUALIFY YOU FOR WHAT'S
NEXT."

Points to Ponder

Write down where you currently are in regard to your ministry, career, and personal relationships. How can you manage each of those areas better so that you can be prepared for the next season of your life?

_____

_____

_____

_____

_____

_____

Day 78

"TOO MANY ARE LOOKING FOR WHAT'S NEXT WITHOUT BEING FAITHFUL WITH WHAT'S *NOW*! BE A GOOD STEWARD OF YOUR *NOW* AND WATCH GOD MOVE LIKE NEVER BEFORE!"

Points to Ponder

What is God trusting you with RIGHT NOW? Are you handling that assignment in faithfulness and as a good steward?

_____

_____

_____

_____

_____

_____

Day 79

"MY WISE MOTHER SAID SOMETHING TO ME THAT GAVE ME SO MUCH PEACE. SHE SAID, 'SON, ST. PAUL WILL BE FINE BECAUSE YOU ARE LEADING THEM TO BECOME A PRAYING PEOPLE. PRAYING CHURCHES NEVER GO UNDER. GOD BLESSES THEM.'"

Points to Ponder

Make a commitment to increase your time and effectiveness in prayer with God. Make a list of those things you are committed to taking before God in prayer and intercession.

_____

_____

_____

_____

_____

_____

Day 80

"KNOW THAT WHEN YOU ARE IN A **PRAYING CHURCH,** THINGS HAPPEN! I'M THANKING GOD FOR A CHURCH THAT LIVES TO PRAY."

Points to Ponder

How do you contribute to the culture of prayer at your church? How can you become more involved in a prayer community?

_____

_____

_____

_____

_____

_____

Day 81

"TAKE YOUR FINGER OFF THE PANIC BUTTON AND CHOOSE TO **TRUST** GOD!"

Points to Ponder

Trusting God is a process. Take some time to write down the areas of your life in which your faith needs to be greater so that you can have fewer moments of panic.

_____

_____

_____

_____

_____

_____

Day 82

"PURSUING THE PURITY OF
HIS PRESENCE MUST BE
ENOUGH TO PUSH YOU PASS
THE PAIN WHICH IS DESIGNED
TO BREAK YOU."

Points to Ponder

Do you spend quality time worshipping God?
What plan do you have in place that will assist
you in pursuing God's presence?

_____

_____

_____

_____

_____

_____

Day 83

"YOUR GREATEST SEASON
WILL NOT BE BASED UPON
WHAT YOU HAVE; IT WILL BE
BASED UPON HOW MUCH FAITH
YOU HAVE TO MOVE FORWARD
WITH LIMITED RESOURCES
WHILE SERVING AN UNLIMITED
GOD."

Points to Ponder

Today, put ALL of your faith in God concerning your destiny. List some of those things.

_____

_____

_____

_____

_____

_____

Day 84

"DECLARE IT: NO MORE DELAY!"

Points to Ponder

Make a declaration that there is no delay in the accomplishment of your goals. Write down your vision or business plan and do something everyday to press forward.

_____

_____

_____

_____

_____

_____

Day 85

"DON'T ALLOW WHAT YOU ARE
EXPERIENCING EXTERNALLY
TO INTERNALLY DICTATE THE
LEVEL OR QUALITY OF YOUR
THOUGHTS."

Points to Ponder

No matter what you may be facing, do your best to think positively. List some positive thoughts and commit to declaring them on a consistent basis.

_____

_____

_____

_____

_____

_____

Day 86

"WIN THE BATTLE OF THE MIND BY SPEAKING THE WORD OF GOD!"

Points to Ponder

To which scriptures do you refer on topics of faith and healing? Write them down and simply speak them into the atmosphere.

_____

_____

_____

_____

_____

_____

Day 87

"EVERY TIME YOU PRAY, YOU REMOVE THE MYSTERY OF GOD."

Points to Ponder

Prayer is essential to us developing a greater relationship with God. Set up some consistent times to pray, and write down the times that you will commit to.

_____

_____

_____

_____

_____

_____

Day 88

"REST IN THE FACT THAT GOD KNOWS YOUR HEART."

Points to Ponder

When you have a pure heart, there is no need to worry. List some of the things that cause you to worry and commit to trusting that God has already taken care of them.

_____

_____

_____

_____

_____

_____

Day 89

"KEEP SOWING!
Harvest is coming!"

Points to Ponder

Write down the names of the people around you who you can sow good seeds into. Seeds can be money, time, a word of encouragement, etc.

_____

_____

_____

_____

_____

_____

Day 90

"GETTING BACK UP IS NOT AN OPTION—IT'S YOUR ASSIGNMENT."

Points to Ponder

What are some of the things you have experienced that you need to bounce back from in order to fulfill your assignment? Write them down and BELIEVE that you WILL rebound!

_____

_____

_____

_____

_____

_____

Day 91

"DON'T SETTLE IN A SEASON THAT IS BENEATH YOU."

Points to Ponder

Even when you experience a difficult season, make the commitment to not settle for less than God desires for you. What is your ultimate goal spiritually, personally, and professionally?

_____

_____

_____

_____

_____

_____

Day 92

"GOD IS SETTING YOU UP FOR GREAT VICTORY."

Points to Ponder

God desires for you to walk in the victory that He has promised you. Write down some of the keys to enjoying victory in Christ.

_____

_____

_____

_____

_____

_____

Day 93

"VICTORY IS **POSSIBLE!** SUCCESS IS **POSSIBLE!** FULFILLMENT IS **POSSIBLE!!** AND GOD IS THE **SOURCE** OF IT ALL!"

Points to Ponder

Are you TRUSTING that God is your source? If not, what hinders you from doing so?

_____

_____

_____

_____

_____

_____

Day 94

"PRAYER PUSHES US INTO MANIFESTATION."

Points to Ponder

Prayer is one of the keys to unlocking manifestation. How committed are you to consistent prayer?

_____

_____

_____

_____

_____

_____

Day 95

"THE OPPORTUNITIES ARE NEVER BIGGER THAN YOU BECAUSE IT IS GOD WHO EXTENDS THE INVITATION INTO IT. GOD HAS ALREADY PREPARED YOU FOR IT."

Points to Ponder

What opportunities do you have right now that you have trusted God to prepare you for? How are you applying the Word of God to your preparation process?

_____

_____

_____

_____

_____

_____

Day 96

"SOW INTO PEOPLE SPONTANEOUSLY IN ORDER TO RECEIVE AN IMMEDIATE HARVEST."

Points to Ponder

How often do you currently sow into others? What hinders you from sowing into others frequently and without hesitation? Write them and ask God to remedy the hindrance to sowing.

_____

_____

_____

_____

_____

_____

Day 97

"IN MY PRAYER TIME I HEARD, 'SON THE ONLY ONE WHO CAN HINDER WHAT I HAVE FOR YOU IS YOU! GET OUT OF MY WAY BUT STAY IN MY WILL.'"

Points to Ponder

What can you do to make sure that you don't hinder what God has for you?

_____

_____

_____

_____

_____

_____

Day 98

"YOU ARE SO AFRAID TO FAIL
UNTIL YOU ARE TOO
PARALYZED TO TRY. CONQUER
FEAR WITH A FAITH IN GOD
WHO IS TRUSTING YOU WITH A
LIFE OF GREAT
POSSIBILITIES."

Points to Ponder

Write down situations where fear prevented
you from trying. Once you write them down,
turn them completely over to God in prayer
and ask Him to give you the faith to live out
the possibilities He has for you.

_____

_____

_____

_____

_____

_____

Day 99

"THIS IS YOUR SEASON TO RISE ABOVE FEAR AND PURSUE THE PLAN OF GOD. MOVE FORWARD."

Points to Ponder

How will you conquer any fear that has made you hesitate to move forward?

_____

_____

_____

_____

_____

Day 100

"KNOW THE DIFFERENCE
BETWEEN WHINING AND
PRAYING. WHINING IS
COMPLAINING WITHOUT FAITH.
PRAYING IS COMMUNICATING
IN CONFIDENCE THAT GOD CAN
AND GOD WILL."

Points to Ponder

Have you been whining or praying? Commit to
making sure that the time you spend with God
consists of communicating the confidence that
HE will.

_____

_____

_____

_____

_____

_____

Day 101

"PEOPLE OFTEN ASK CHRISTIANS, 'WHAT MAKES YOU DIFFERENT?' WELL HERE'S MY THOUGHT: WHAT MAKES US DIFFERENT IS THAT GOD CAN TRUST US WITH THE OUTCOME NO MATTER HOW PAINFUL AND CHALLENGING THE PROCESS IS!"

Points to Ponder

Can God trust you with outcomes? How can you ensure that you are a good example of a Christian based on how you handle outcomes and processes?

_____

_____

_____

_____

_____

_____

Day 102

"THE DOORS GOD OPEN FOR YOU
CANNOT BE CLOSED BY ANYONE!
THEIR HANDS AREN'T BIG ENOUGH
TO TURN THE KNOB, NOR ARE
THEY STRONG ENOUGH TO PUSH IT
CLOSED. REST AND WALK
THROUGH IT."

Read Philippians 4:19.

Points to Ponder

Read Philippians 4:19. Rest in the fact that when God opens doors for you, no one can shut them. What are your thoughts?

_____

_____

_____

_____

_____

_____

Day 103

"GIVE GOD A LIFE HE CAN
USE AND WATCH GOD GIVE
YOU A LIFE YOU WILL ENJOY."

Points to Ponder

Are you committed to surrendering your
WHOLE life to God? What would make your
life more enjoyable? Submit it to God and
watch your life transform.

———————————————————

———————————————————

———————————————————

———————————————————

———————————————————

———————————————————

Day 104

"I LOVE SITTING OUTSIDE AT NIGHT.
THE SOUNDS OF NATURE ARE A
WONDERFUL REMINDER THAT GOD
CONTROLS ALL THINGS. I
CHALLENGE YOU TO CONNECT WITH
THE WORLD AND LISTEN! GOD IS
TALKING THROUGH NATURE."

Read Psalms 19:1-6.

Points to Ponder

Read Psalms 19:1-6. In what ways and how often can you connect with nature in order to hear God speaking?

_____

_____

_____

_____

_____

_____

Day 105

"WHAT ENABLES US TO
ACCOMPLISH THE AMAZING
PLAN OF GOD?
SIMPLY STATED: CONFIDENCE.
A CONFIDENCE THAT WON'T
NEGOTIATE NO MATTER WHAT
THE EXTERNAL REALITIES
SUGGEST."

Points to Ponder

Is your confidence in God or is your
confidence in man? Read Philippians 4:13 and
identify some ways in which you can place
more confidence in God alone.

_____

_____

_____

_____

_____

_____

Day 106

"CONFIDENCE SUBDUES FEAR AND
REFUSES TO CONVERSE WITH
INTIMIDATION. THIS CONFIDENCE
IS THE RESULT OF A MARRIAGE
BETWEEN HUMILITY AND
COURAGE. IT FLOWS FROM THE
LIFE OF ONE WHO DARES TO
SUBMIT WITHOUT TREPIDATION.
WALK IT. IT'S YOURS."

Read 1 Samuel 17:45-46.

Points to Ponder

Read 1 Samuel 17:45-46 and summarize how
you can apply what you read to your life.

_____

_____

_____

_____

_____

_____

Day 107

"IT IS AMAZING TO KNOW THAT
GOD HAS OUR LIVES MAPPED
OUT, AND IF WE WILL
OPERATE ACCORDING TO HIS
WORD AND HIS WORKS, ALL
THINGS WILL WORK TOGETHER
FOR OUR GOOD."

Points to Ponder

Read Romans 8:28. Try to find something
positive in a situation you are currently facing
and write it down.

_____

_____

_____

_____

_____

_____

Day 108

"TRUST GOD AND FOLLOW THE PATH HE HAS ORDAINED FOR YOU."

Points to Ponder

Today, take the time to pray and ask God to show you the plan He has for your life. Write down what He reveals to you.

_____

_____

_____

_____

_____

_____

Day 109

"DO IT AGAIN DOUBLE!"

Points to Ponder

We all may experience seasons of loss, but God is able to restore us. Write down those things that you are asking God to "double" in your life.

_____

_____

_____

_____

_____

_____

Day 110

"IF YOU CAN SERVE IN *THAT,* THEN YOU CAN GET THROUGH *THIS*!"

Points to Ponder

Reflect on the times in which you may have faced challenges while serving God. Write down how God brought you through those challenges.

_____

_____

_____

_____

_____

_____

Day 111

"LET YOUR ENEMIES CHASE YOU. THEY CAN'T CATCH YOU."

Points to Ponder

In what ways do you feel like the enemy is after you? Make a commitment to not worrying about it, but rather trusting that God won't let you down.

_____

_____

_____

_____

_____

_____

Day 112

"PROMOTION IS COMING, BUT
HOW DO YOU HANDLE THE
SEASON IN WHICH NOBODY
KNOWS YOU?"

Points to Ponder

How do you handle going through seasons of development?

_____

_____

_____

_____

_____

_____

Day 113

"ONCE YOU FACE YOUR FAILURES, YOU CAN HAVE PEACE."

Points to Ponder

Have you truly faced your failures or times when you may have fallen short? How can you make sure that you always have peace?

_____

_____

_____

_____

_____

_____

Day 114

"DON'T OPEN YOUR MOUTH IF YOU DON'T EXPECT GOD TO ANSWER!"

Points to Ponder

When you ask God for something, do you REALLY believe that He can come through for you? Read Philippians 4:13 and declare that God can do ALL things.

_____

_____

_____

_____

_____

_____

Day 115

"GO THROUGH YOUR SEASON OF AUTHENTICITY! DON'T COMPROMISE!"

Points to Ponder

What has God allowed you to experience to bring you closer to Him and to give you a greater perspective of who He has called you to be?

Day 116

"YOU MUST COURAGEOUSLY FIGHT AGAINST YOUR INSECURITIES."

Points to Ponder

Identify any areas of your life in which you may struggle with insecurities, and list them. Pray about how you can gradually overcome each one.

_____

_____

_____

_____

_____

_____

Day 117

"GOD WILL KEEP YOU UNTIL HE CHANGES YOUR STORY."

Points to Ponder

Write down some experiences you have had where you know it was only God that got you through it.

_____

_____

_____

_____

_____

_____

Day 118

"I TRUST GOD TOO MUCH TO
PUT A NUMBER ON WHAT I
CONSIDER TO BE A
PRIVILEGE."

Points to Ponder

Serving God is an honor and a privilege. Make a list of the various gifts and talents that God has blessed you to have, and make a commitment to ensuring that He gets the glory from them.

_____

_____

_____

_____

_____

_____

Day 119

"TRUST THE GIFT OF GOD RATHER THAN THE GIFT OF PEOPLE."

Points to Ponder

Read Proverbs 3: 5-6 and commit to placing a greater level of trust in Him. List some of the ways that God has gifted you, and give thanks for each of them.

_____

_____

_____

_____

_____

_____

Day 120

"GOD WILL GIVE YOU THE DESIRED OUTCOME BY TRANSCENDING YOUR EXPECTATIONS."

Points to Ponder

List moments where God has given you above and beyond what you needed or even asked Him for. As you reflect on them, have the faith to believe that He can and will do it again!

_____

_____

_____

_____

_____

_____

Day 121

"NEVER WORSHIP WHAT GOD
HAS A REMEDY FOR. GOD
SECURES US THROUGH
COMFORT."

Points to Ponder

Have you ever had an experience that was so
overwhelming that you made it more powerful
than it actually was? Make a commitment to
praying and trusting God more—knowing that
He is GREATER than anything that you may
ever face.

_____

_____

_____

_____

_____

_____

Day 122

"WHEN YOU HAVE PEACE, YOU'RE REMINDED THAT GOD IS ON THE THRONE."

Points to Ponder

What does having peace mean to you? Based on the definition you gave, do you feel that you truly have peace? Write down some of the things that you can do to ensure that you have peace.

_____

_____

_____

_____

_____

_____

Day 123

"CAN YOU HANDLE BEING HURT DURING YOUR PROCESS FOR THE SAKE OF BEING PERMANENTLY HEALED LATER?"

Points to Ponder

How committed to the process are you? What would keep you from turning away if you are ever up against hurt or pain?

_____

_____

_____

_____

_____

_____

Day 124

"WORK THE PROCESS EVEN IF YOUR CONDITIONS ARE NOT CONDUCIVE."

Points to Ponder

What conditions are you facing that may not be conducive? How will you ensure that you stay faithful to your process despite the fact that your conditions may not be comfortable?

_____

_____

_____

_____

_____

_____

Day 125

"IF GOD ORCHESTRATES A DRY SEASON IN YOUR LIFE, DON'T WORRY. WHEREVER HE LEADS YOU IS **ALREADY** PREGNANT WITH EVERYTHING YOU NEED."

Points to Ponder

Have you ever experienced a dry season? Name some of the ways that God STILL makes provisions for you even when the season is dry.

_____

_____

_____

_____

_____

_____

Day 126

"YOU CAN'T BE A GIANT IN PRAISE BUT A MIDGET IN FAITH."

Points to Ponder

Make a consistent effort to make sure that your faith level is as high as your praise level. What are your thoughts on how you can better exercise your faith?

_____

_____

_____

_____

_____

_____

Day 127

"IN ORDER TO GET TO THE
NEXT LEVEL, WE MUST OPEN
OUR HEARTS TO THE
POSSIBILITIES OF THE NEW
THINGS GOD WANTS TO
INTRODUCE US TO."

Points to Ponder

How can you become more open to
EVERYTHING God may want to introduce
you to in order to get you to the next level?

_____

_____

_____

_____

_____

_____

Day 128

"GOD IS TURNING THIS IN YOUR FAVOR."

Points to Ponder

Do you have the faith to believe that God is turning around every unfavorable situation that you face? Write down the things that you need God to turn around, and make the declaration that it's already done!

_____

_____

_____

_____

_____

_____

Day 129

"IT'S RIGHT THERE. DON'T BLOW THIS!"

Points to Ponder

What opportunities do you have right now that you can't afford to miss? List them and put your faith and strength in God to lead you in the right direction.

_____

_____

_____

_____

_____

_____

Day 130

"DON'T BE SO DEEP IN THE PAIN THAT YOU CAN'T APPROACH GOD WITH A PURE HEART."

Points to Ponder

When you approach God, are you doing it with a pure heart? If not, what painful experiences have you had that you need to authentically heal from?

Day 131

"MANY OF US MISS OUR SEASON BECAUSE WE ARE FOCUSED ON OUR PROBLEMS."

Points to Ponder

We ALL have problems, but we can't allow them to cause us to miss our season. What problems do you have that you need to turn over to God? Read Psalm 55:22 and declare that your problems are on the shoulders of the Lord!

_____

_____

_____

_____

_____

_____

Day 132

"SOMETIMES IT'S NOT MY SITUATION THAT NEEDS TO GET BETTER—IT'S ME."

Points to Ponder

Are you committed to becoming BETTER? Take some time to write down some things about your personality or character that needs improvement for you to live an even greater life for God.

_____

_____

_____

_____

_____

_____

Day 133

"CAN YOU HANDLE
PROMOTION WHEN PROMOTION
IS DEMOTION? WHAT IF GOD
HAS TO BRING YOU DOWN IN
ORDER TO BRING YOU UP TO
SIZE?"

Points to Ponder

Have you experienced a demotion that actually turned out to be promotion? How did you handle it initially? How will you handle demotion in the future if you ever have to experience it again?

_____

_____

_____

_____

_____

_____

147

Day 134

"ABRAHAM'S FAITH HAD TO MATCH THE PROMISE."

Points to Ponder

What has God promised you that will require your faith level to increase?

_____

_____

_____

_____

_____

_____

Day 135

"I'M A WITNESS THAT GOD WILL COVER YOU AND PROMOTE YOU THROUGH IT ALL!"

Points to Ponder

How has God covered you despite some of the negative experiences or situations you have faced?

_____

_____

_____

_____

_____

_____

Day 136

"DON'T LOSE HEART. THE DOORS ARE OPENING FOR YOU IF YOU TRUST GOD AND NEVER DOUBT."

Points to Ponder

What do you do when doubt creeps into your mind? Discipline yourself to pray before you find yourself losing heart or faith.

_____

_____

_____

_____

_____

_____

Day 137

"IF YOU KEEP WALKING EVEN
WHEN THE DOOR IS CLOSED TO
YOU, YOUR FAITH WILL GIVE
GOD THE AUTHORITY TO OPEN
IT BEFORE YOU GET THERE."

Points to Ponder

Are there doors that seem to be closed that you
are believing for God to open? Write them
down and ask God to open them!

_____

_____

_____

_____

_____

_____

Day 138

"Obey and take your hands off!"

Points to Ponder

Is there anything that God has instructed you to take your hands off of but you still find yourself holding on? Today, make a commitment to give those things completely to God.

_____

_____

_____

_____

_____

_____

Day 139

"WHEREVER GOD ASSIGNS ME, THAT'S WHERE HE IS GOING TO BLESS ME."

Points to Ponder

Do you have faith to believe that wherever God assigns you is where He is going to bless you? Take some time to write down the people, places, and things that God has assigned you to in this season and declare that you are BLESSED!

_____

_____

_____

_____

_____

_____

Day 140

"WATCH GOD MEET YOUR NEED OR MAKE YOU GREATER THAN YOUR NEED."

Points to Ponder

List those things that you need God to make you "greater than." During your prayer time, declare them in His presence.

_____

_____

_____

_____

_____

_____

Day 141

"GOD IS PLACING YOU IN A POSITION OF FAVOR!"

Points to Ponder

Write down every area of your life in which you need the favor of God.

_____

_____

_____

_____

_____

_____

Day 142

"GOD DOESN'T PROVIDE IN STAGNATION; HE PROVIDES WHEN YOU'RE OBEDIENT."

Points to Ponder

What areas of your life are stagnant? How will you make the necessary adjustments to obey God so that He can provide?

_____

_____

_____

_____

_____

_____

Day 143

"ALL GOD REQUIRES IS THAT YOU DO WHAT HE SAYS AND OBEY."

Points to Ponder

Do whatever is necessary to ensure that you are living a life in obedience to God. What are some things that hinder you from total obedience?

_____

_____

_____

_____

_____

_____

Day 144

"IF I DO WHAT I KNOW TO DO AND BE OBEDIENT, GOD WILL TAKE CARE OF THE REST."

Points to Ponder

Rest in God today and have the confidence that He will take care of those things that concern you. Make a list of some of those things.

_____

_____

_____

_____

_____

_____

Day 145

"GOD IS GOING TO BLESS YOU RIGHT WHERE YOU ARE!"

Points to Ponder

Read Deuteronomy 28:6 and declare that you are blessed right where you are!

—————————————————

—————————————————

—————————————————

—————————————————

—————————————————

—————————————————

Day 146

"WHEN YOU SERVE AND HONOR GOD IN ADVERSITY, GOD CAN TURN IT."

Points to Ponder

Are you facing adversity? How will you continue to serve God in the midst of the adversity that you may face?

_____

_____

_____

_____

_____

_____

Day 147

"GOD WILL BLESS YOU WHEN YOU COMMIT TO THE PROCESS AND PURPOSE."

Points to Ponder

Have you made a consistent commitment to process and purpose? Write down what you feel your purpose is and spend some time praying concerning the process God wants to take you through in order to get there.

_____

_____

_____

_____

_____

_____

Day 148

"EVEN WHEN YOU DON'T LIKE IT, STAY FAITHFUL IN THE EXPERIENCE."

Points to Ponder

What are you currently going through that you don't like? Develop a strategy for how you will stay the course and go through it so that the experience can be used to glorify God later.

_____

_____

_____

_____

_____

_____

Day 149

"DELAY DOESN'T MEAN
DENIAL. GOD IS JUST
DEVELOPING YOU FOR A
BIGGER HARVEST."

Points to Ponder

List the things that you have been believing
God to do for you but seem as though they
may be delayed. Trust and declare that God is
simply developing you for a bigger harvest.

_____

_____

_____

_____

_____

_____

Day 150

"GOD IS ABOUT TO GIVE YOU A SECOND CHANCE. THE PERSON WHO WALKS IN IT THIS TIME WILL BE FAR DIFFERENT THAN THE PERSON WHO WALKED IN IT THE LAST TIME."

Points to Ponder

Every now and then, we are all in need of a second chance. Write down one area of your life in which you are trusting God to allow you to try again, and declare that you will be victorious once He does.

_____

_____

_____

_____

_____

_____

Day 151

"GOD IS ABOUT TO ELEVATE YOU AND EVERYTHING AROUND YOU."

Points to Ponder

Do you truly believe that God is able to elevate you and the things around you? Read Philippians 1:6 and make the declaration that God is completing the good work that he started within you!

_____

_____

_____

_____

_____

Vitamin C

COVENANT WITH GOD

Covenant with God

We are built to be relational. Regardless of how painful and disappointing relationships have been, we are DESIGNED for covenant. That's the way God created us. It is clear that this is the Infinite Intellect's purpose because in Genesis 1:27 and Genesis 2, God frames creation around covenant. God creates humanity and then gives the non-negotiable directive to "be fruitful and multiply." This directive is ONLY achieved through covenant. This one cannot claim to be fully human without being actively engaged in covenant.

To ensure that you are moving forward positively, let me define covenant. It is an agreement between two unique and distinct people or parties. It is about the building and maintenance of bridges where persons engage each other in a healthy, Godly way. The goal is always that each party is fully respected and is better for the existence of the relationship. Because of that, ALL healthy relationships should be birthed out of our covenant with God.

In essence, we do not begin with each other; we begin with God. Relationship with God (which is built on faith) becomes the foundation of every relationship in our lives. As well, it becomes the standard for evaluating relationship(s) that should not intrude upon the one we have with God. Covenant with God shapes our sense of self and propels us into a world of wounded people whom we are capable of loving and forgiving.

The value of Vitamin C is so important to your personal growth that it cannot be measured. Vitamin C is designed to enhance your spiritual growth by strengthening your covenant relationship with God who continues to pursue you through Jesus Christ. These insightful thoughts, as they are digested, will give you direction as it relates to living a productive, prosperous Godly life. You will find yourself seeking God daily—craving God while maturing in your love for others. You will consecrate time for God and God alone. In the end, you will discover the amazing peace that can only be yours when in covenant with God.

Day 152

"SIN OF A PREVIOUS SEASON IS TURNING INTO SALVATION IN A NEW SEASON."

Points to Ponder

What sin from your previous seasons are you willing to use as testimonies of your salvation? What do you need to do personally to make that this happens?

_____

_____

_____

_____

_____

_____

Day 153

"HUMILITY IS A REQUIRED INGREDIENT FOR KINGDOM GREATNESS. NEVER BE FOOLED BY THOSE WHO HAVE A TEMPORARY SEASON OF SUCCESS WITHOUT HUMILITY."

Read Luke 14:11.

Points to Ponder

Are you practicing the trait of humility consistently? Name some of the areas of your life in which you know that you can demonstrate a greater level of humility.

_____

_____

_____

_____

_____

_____

Day 154

"MARRY YOUR PERSON TO HIS PURPOSE."

Points to Ponder

Have you identified your purpose in life? Once you do, make the commitment to aligning who you are with what you are called to become.

_____

_____

_____

_____

_____

_____

Day 155

"SEEK THE LORD ABOUT ANY
AREA OF YOUR LIFE THAT
MAKES YOUR WITNESS
UNATTRACTIVE."

Points to Ponder

What areas of your life are making your witness
unattractive? Strive to seek God for direction
on how to become as attractive of a witness as
possible!

_____

_____

_____

_____

_____

_____

Day 156

"ONE'S PERCEPTION
DETERMINES HOW ONE
RELATES TO GOD. IT IS ALSO
THE DETERMINING FACTOR
FOR WHAT YOU RECEIVE FROM
GOD."

Points to Ponder

How is your current perception of God
affecting how you relate to Him? Is that
perception limiting what you can receive from
Him?

_____

_____

_____

_____

_____

_____

Day 157

"DO NOT WALK HER DOWN THE AISLE IF YOU DO NOT HAVE A VISION FOR HER."

Points to Ponder

Do you currently have a vision for the people closely connected to you? What commitments will you make to ensure that the vision is developed and carried out?

_____

_____

_____

_____

_____

_____

Day 158

"LOVE YOUR WIFE SO SHE IS BEAUTIFIED BY YOUR LOVE."

Points to Ponder

List some ways that you could love your spouse so that he/she is illuminated by it?

_____

_____

_____

_____

_____

_____

Day 159

"DISCERN YOUR RELATIONSHIPS AND STOP CONNECTING TO PEOPLE WITH BROKEN SPIRITS."

Points to Ponder

Who have you connected to that had a broken spirit? What will you do to make sure that the connections you make in the future are with people that are whole in spirit?

_____

_____

_____

_____

_____

_____

Day 160

"GOD IS TIRED OF YOU LOSING STUFF HE'S BLESSED YOU WITH BECAUSE OF WHO YOU'RE CONNECTED TO."

Read Psalms 1:1.

Points to Ponder

Read Psalm 1:1 and write down how you will apply this scripture to your personal walk with Jesus Christ.

_____

_____

_____

_____

_____

_____

Day 161

"DEVELOP A PRAYER LIFE—
NOT JUST MOMENTS WHEN
YOU PRAY. YOUR
CONSISTENCY WILL PRODUCE
THE GODLY RESPONSE YOU
DESIRE."

Read Luke 5:16.

Points to Ponder

Write down a plan for a consistent prayer life so that God can produce the greatest results in your life.

_____

_____

_____

_____

_____

_____

Day 162

"MARRIAGE IS THE ONLY
RELATIONSHIP THAT JESUS
SAYS LOOKS LIKE HIM, SO THE
CHURCH MUST PROTECT IT
AND STOP DEVALUING THE
SANCTITY OF IT."

Points to Ponder

If you are married or have the desire to be married, what are ways to ensure that the relationship will look like Him? Read Ephesians 5:22-33.

_____

_____

_____

_____

_____

_____

Day 163

"WHEN GOD KNOWS YOUR
HEART, HE CUTS YOU A BREAK
WITH GRACE."

Points to Ponder

Write about an experience where you committed a sin but God gave you grace because He knew your heart was pure.

_____

_____

_____

_____

_____

_____

Day 164

"GROWTH IS EVIDENT WHEN OBEDIENCE IS OBVIOUS."

Points to Ponder

Give an example of a time when you obeyed God and your maturity in that obedience inspired someone else.

_____

_____

_____

_____

_____

_____

Day 165

"OBEDIENCE PRODUCES WHAT PERFORMANCE CAN'T."

Points to Ponder

Make a commitment to living a life of obedience so that you can go further than your performance can take you.

_____

_____

_____

_____

_____

_____

Day 166

"PROMOTION IS THE QUALIFIED STAGE OF BEING POSITIONED IN ASSIGNMENT."

Points to Ponder

Where has God positioned you that's preparing you for your next promotion?

_____

_____

_____

_____

_____

_____

Day 167

"WOW! JUST HEARD A MAJOR STATEMENT: IF THE CHURCHES AROUND YOU ARE GROWING, IT WILL HELP YOUR CHURCH GROW. GOD HAS CALLED US TO BE PARTNERS!!! WE MUST AID EACH OTHER AND NOT COMPETE."

Points to Ponder

Are you partnering effectively with the people that God has put around you? How can your partnership with them improve?

_____

_____

_____

_____

_____

_____

Day 168

"FATHER: CLEANSE OUR HEARTS OF ANYTHING THAT MISDIRECTS OUR FOCUS, CAUSES US TO MISMANAGE OUR ASSIGNMENT, OR INDUCES US TO MISUSE OUR WORDS."

Points to Ponder

Is there anything in your life that consistently causes you to mismanage your assignment? If so, identify what it is and ask God to cleanse your heart of it.

_____

_____

_____

_____

_____

_____

Day 169

"Declare it: I'm saved and my future is secure!"

Points to Ponder

Have the faith in God to believe that you are saved by His grace and mercy. Read Romans 8:38-39 and write a reflection.

_____

_____

_____

_____

_____

_____

Day 170

"I'M A FIRM BELIEVER THAT ANY
CHURCH THAT HONORS, AND
RESPECTS AND VALUES THEIR
PASTOR WILL EXPERIENCE GOD'S
VALUE UNIQUELY. COMMIT TO
HONORING YOUR MAN OR WOMAN OF
GOD. THERE'S A BLESSING IN
HONORING YOUR LEADER."

Read Hebrews 13:17.

Points to Ponder

How can you do a better job of showing your leader(s) honor?

_____

_____

_____

_____

_____

_____

Day 171

"LET'S MOVE FROM SEASONS
OF CONSECRATION TO A LIFE
OF CONSECRATION.
FATHER: CLEANSE OUR
HEARTS. WE ONLY WANT TO
PLEASE YOU."

Psalms 19:12.

Points to Ponder

What adjustment can you make spiritually to
ensure that you live a consecrated life?

_____

_____

_____

_____

_____

_____

Day 172

"YOUNGER PREACHERS OFTEN ASK ME FOR ADVICE AND THE BEST I CAN TELL THEM AFTER 30 YEARS IS: SEEK TO LIVE HOLY, HUMBLE AND ACCOUNTABLE TO GOD."

Points to Ponder

Are you living the best quality of life that you possibly can? How can you create a lifestyle that is more holy, humble, and accountable unto God?

_____

_____

_____

_____

_____

_____

Day 173

"MY PASSION IS TO BECOME A
MAN WITH A PURE AND
UNDEFILED HEART."

Points to Ponder

Strive to have a pure heart. Write down some of the challenges we face that may cause our hearts to become impure. How will you respond to those challenges so that you can maintain a pure heart at all times?

_____

_____

_____

_____

_____

_____

Day 174

"I WANT NOTHING TO STAND BETWEEN ME AND GOD. FATHER: EXPOSE ME TO ME!"

Points to Ponder

Are you willing to allow God to expose you to yourself so that nothing can stand between you and Him? What has he revealed thus far?

_____

_____

_____

_____

_____

_____

Day 175

"THERE'S NOTHING WORSE THAN MEETING YOUR SPOUSE AFTER THE WEDDING."

Points to Ponder

How can you make a commitment to having a healthy relationship from the very beginning? What are some ways to get to know someone on a deeper level?

_____

_____

_____

_____

_____

_____

Day 176

"SOMEBODY THOUGHT THEY
COULD DESTROY YOU, BUT
GOD DECIDED TO MUTE THE
ENEMY IN ORDER TO PROTECT
YOUR DESTINY."

Points to Ponder

Think of a time when God protected you from the destruction of the enemy. Make a consistent effort to believe that no matter what happens, God will protect your destiny.

_____

_____

_____

_____

_____

_____

Day 177

"DON'T GET SO CAUGHT UP IN MOVING THE CHURCH SYSTEM THAT YOU FORGET THE SAVIOR."

Points to Ponder

Read Matthew 6:33 and describe how it relates to keeping God first in everything, including the everyday movement of the church and the ministry.

_____

_____

_____

_____

_____

_____

Day 178

"CAN YOU BLESS SOMEONE WHO MAY NOT BE ABLE TO BLESS YOU?"

Points to Ponder

Have you ever taken the time to be a blessing to someone that either couldn't be a blessing to you or didn't have a desire to? What are the benefits of being a blessing to other people?

_____

_____

_____

_____

_____

_____

Day 179

"NEVER COMPARE YOURSELF
TO THOSE WHO DOESN'T HAVE
THE STANDARD OF JESUS
CHRIST IN THEIR LIVES."

Points to Ponder

The comparison trap is easy to fall into. Have
you ever made the mistake of comparing
yourself to other people? What adjustments
have you made to not allow yourself to fall into
the comparison trap?

_____

_____

_____

_____

_____

_____

Day 180

"DON'T ABORT YOUR NEXT
SEASON BY HAVING
UNNECESSARY BLOOD ON
YOUR HANDS."

Points to Ponder

What situation have you considered putting
your hands on but God instructed you to let it
go?

_____

_____

_____

_____

_____

_____

Day 181

"AT THE END OF THE DAY, YOU
WANT TO FEEL THE HEART OF
GOD."

Points to Ponder

Are you constructing your life and the things
around you so that you can authentically feel
the heart of God?

_____

_____

_____

_____

_____

_____

Day 182

"A REAL WORSHIPER DOESN'T
DEMAND THE PRESENCE OF
PEOPLE. A REAL WORSHIPER
DEMANDS THE PRESENCE OF
GOD."

Points to Ponder

Make a conscious and consistent effort to pursue the presence of God during your times of worship. How can you minimize distractions?

_____

_____

_____

_____

_____

_____

Day 183

"GOD MAY GIVE THE DEVIL ACCESS, BUT HE NEVER GIVES HIM AUTHORITY."

Points to Ponder

Write down an example of a time you experienced a trial but God reminded you that HE is still in authority.

_____

_____

_____

_____

_____

_____

Day 184

"IF YOU DON'T LOVE YOURSELF, YOU CAN NEVER TRULY LOVE ANYONE ELSE. THAT'S WHY SOME PEOPLE WHO ARE MARRIED WILL ONLY BE ROOMMATES."

Points to Ponder

Have you taken the time to love yourself? Are you spending enough time with God for Him to show you who you are in Him?

_____

_____

_____

_____

_____

_____

Day 185

"LEADERSHIP IN THE KINGDOM ISN'T AUTHORITY— IT'S SERVICE."

Points to Ponder

What commitments have you made to serving? Write down how you will be a more faithful servant in your ministry, in your place of employment, and even within your community.

_____

_____

_____

_____

_____

_____

Day 186

"ANYTHING THAT CONTROLS YOUR BEHAVIOR OTHER THAN GOD IS AN IDOL."

Points to Ponder

Does anything in your life have your attention more than God does? If so, make an effort today to make God your primary priority.

_____

_____

_____

_____

_____

_____

Day 187

"IS THE CHURCH VISIBLE WITHOUT THE BUILDING?"

Points to Ponder

How are you representing God's church as an individual? Write down some of the things that you are committed to doing to make sure that the people around you can see that you are a part of God's church.

_____

_____

_____

_____

_____

_____

Day 188

"THE SPIRIT OF REBELLION ALWAYS MAKES YOU LOOK BAD—NEVER GOOD."

Points to Ponder

How has rebellion caused you to look bad in the past? How have you matured to overcome moments when it seems like rebellion is convenient?

_____

_____

_____

_____

_____

_____

Day 189

"YOUR JOB IS TO BE A CONFESSOR AND LET PEOPLE KNOW THAT GOD DID IT!"

Points to Ponder

Commit yourself to positive, daily confessions concerning the fact that God is able! Start today by writing down some of the amazing things He has done and the things that He will do.

_____

_____

_____

_____

_____

_____

Day 190

"GOD WILL NEVER ALLOW YOU TO BE COMFORTABLE WITH THAT PART OF YOU THAT SIN CREATED."

Points to Ponder

What parts of your life are becoming more uncomfortable as you get closer and closer to God? Explain some of the ways He is cleansing you.

_____

_____

_____

_____

_____

_____

Day 191

"DON'T SHOUT WHEN GOD BRINGS YOU OUT. SHOUT WHILE HE KEEPS YOU IN IT!"

Points to Ponder

What situation are you right now that God desires for you to rejoice in before He brings you out?

_____

_____

_____

_____

_____

_____

Day 192

"GOD WILL NOT ALLOW YOU TO GO UNDER."

Points to Ponder

No matter what you face, have the confidence that God will always keep you. Declare it!

_____

_____

_____

_____

_____

_____

Day 193

"MARRY SOMEONE YOU'RE
WILLING MAKE GODLY
CHANGES FOR SO THAT GOD
CAN HONOR WHO YOU
BECOME."

Points to Ponder

How have you committed in your heart to
make Godly changes for the spouse that God
has given you (or will give you)?

_____

_____

_____

_____

_____

_____

Day 194

"IF A COUPLE HAS A DISAGREEMENT, WHO CARES WHO WINS THE ARGUMENT IF THERE'S ONLY TWO PEOPLE IN THE ROOM."

Points to Ponder

Who are you arguing with that you should actually spend more time partnering with? How will you make sure that you spend less time arguing and more time partnering?

_____

_____

_____

_____

_____

_____

Day 195

"MANY PEOPLE ARE DEFEATED
BECAUSE THEY DON'T SPEND
ENOUGH TIME THINKING
ABOUT ALL THAT GOD HAS
DONE—OR TO THE POINT
WHERE IT CAUSES THEM TO
THANK HIM."

Points to Ponder

Take the time today to simply THANK God
for ALL that He has done. Write down a list
of things that you can thank Him for and begin
doing it!

_____

_____

_____

_____

_____

_____

Day 196

"TODAY, LOOK AROUND YOU
AND LEARN FROM OTHERS
WHOSE MISTAKES CAN BE
TEACHING TOOLS."

Points to Ponder

Are you observing mistakes that are being made by the people close to you? How can you use their mistakes as teaching tools?

_____

_____

_____

_____

_____

_____

Day 197

"UNDISCIPLINED BEHAVIOR CAN COST YOU EVERYTHING."

Points to Ponder

Have you ever had an experience where a lack of disciplined behavior cost you something? What are you doing now to create a greater level of discipline?

_____

_____

_____

_____

_____

_____

Day 198

"STRIVE TO BRING EVERY AREA OF YOUR LIFE UNDER THE AUTHORITY OF JESUS CHRIST."

Points to Ponder

Make the commitment to bring every area of your life under the authority of Jesus Christ.

_____

_____

_____

_____

_____

_____

Day 199

"THE WORDS THAT COME OUT OF YOUR MOUTH, THE THINGS YOU POST ON SOCIAL MEDIA, THE SEXUAL SITUATIONS YOU ENTER INTO, THE VENTING SESSIONS YOU HAVE, AND ANYTHING ELSE YOU DO THAT DOESN'T HONOR GOD CAN COST YOU."

Points to Ponder

Is there anything going on in your life right now that doesn't honor God? What adjustments can you make to honor God more?

_____

_____

_____

_____

_____

_____

Day 200

"DON'T TRY TO DIRECT THE CHURCH WHEN YOU ARE NOT DIRECTED BY THE SPIRIT."

Points to Ponder

In what ways can you be led by the Spirit in order to effectively lead others?

_____

_____

_____

_____

_____

_____

Day 201

"COUNTENANCE CALLS
OTHERS TO HAVE CONFIDENCE
IN GOD."

Points to Ponder

Does your countenance cause the people that
meet you to have more confidence in God?

_____

_____

_____

_____

_____

_____

Day 202

"FOCUS ON THE FATHER, NOT THE FAILURES."

Points to Ponder

Read Psalm 46:1 and make Jesus Christ your focus rather than any failure that you have experienced.

_____

_____

_____

_____

_____

_____

Day 203

"DECLARE IT: MY FAMILY IS BLESSED!"

Points to Ponder

Write down the names of your family members—no matter how immediate or distant they are. Declare that they are BLESSED!

_____

_____

_____

_____

_____

_____

Day 204

"YOUR SEED SHALL PROSPER AND BE GREAT!"

Points to Ponder

Have the confidence in God that your seed will become ALL that He desires for it to be. Take a moment to reflect.

_____

_____

_____

_____

_____

_____

Day 205

"SPEAK LIFE OVER YOUR CHILDREN."

Points to Ponder

Name the children that you cover in any way. Write out a positive confession concerning them and declare it consistently.

_____

_____

_____

_____

_____

_____

Day 206

"SET YOUR SEED UP FOR GREATNESS."

Points to Ponder

What decisions are you making today that will set your children up for greatness? What doors will your name allow them to walk through?

_____

_____

_____

_____

_____

_____

Day 207

"ADMIT ADVERSITY AND YOUR WRONGDOINGS."

Points to Ponder

Have you (or a loved one) ever gone through adversity as a result of things you may have done wrong? Make the commitment to admit your wrong doings so that you can go through adversity victoriously and so that others may heal.

_____

_____

_____

_____

_____

_____

Day 208

"AS LONG AS I AM IN THE WILL OF GOD, I AM IN THE PROVISION OF GOD."

Points to Ponder

Seek God today concerning His will for your life. What is the evidence that you are in His will?

_____

_____

_____

_____

_____

_____

Day 209

"IF YOUR FAITH MATCHES YOUR OBEDIENCE, AND YOUR OBEDIENCE MATCHES YOUR FAITH, THERE IS NOTHING GOD WON'T DO FOR YOU AND THROUGH YOU."

Points to Ponder

In what ways can you improve your level of obedience? Your level of faith?

_____

_____

_____

_____

_____

_____

Day 210

"SOW WHEN YOU'RE IN FAMINE."

Points to Ponder

Commit to sowing consistently, especially when you experience a famine. How can you overcome the fear of not having enough?

_____

_____

_____

_____

_____

_____

Day 211

"WE WANT THE PERKS BUT WE DON'T WANT THE PRESENCE."

Points to Ponder

Are you just as hungry for the presence of God as you are the perks that come with being a child of God? How can you differentiate between your love for the gift and your love for the Giver.

_____

_____

_____

_____

_____

_____

Day 212

"STOP SENDING GOD MIXED SIGNALS CONCERNING YOUR LIFESTYLE."

Points to Ponder

Does your lifestyle please God? What positive changes can you make to be more pleasing to Him?

_____

_____

_____

_____

_____

_____

Day 213

"EVERYTHING THAT WE NEED AND EVERYTHING THAT WE DESIRE IS TIED TO OBEDIENCE."

Points to Ponder

In what ways are you committed to living a life of obedience?

_____

_____

_____

_____

_____

_____

Day 214

"SOME PEOPLE MAKE COMMITMENTS OUT OF CONVENIENCE RATHER THAN COVENANT."

Points to Ponder

How can you make sure that your commitments are based on a covenant, rather than convenience?

_____

_____

_____

_____

_____

_____

Day 215

"REALIGN YOURSELF WITH THE STANDARD OF GOD."

Points to Ponder

Take some time to read the word of God today and strive to align every area of your life with His word.

_____

_____

_____

_____

_____

_____

Day 216

"ACCEPT CORRECTION AND DON'T JUSTIFY YOUR BEHAVIOR."

Points to Ponder

How do you respond to correction? Is your first response an attempt to justify it? If someone attempts to correct you, simply accept it before you get offended.

_____

_____

_____

_____

_____

_____

Day 217

"CONFESS YOUR SINS AND ADMIT YOU MADE A MISTAKE."

Points to Ponder

Read 1 John 1:9 and become quick to admit when you make a mistake. Write a brief reflection.

_____

_____

_____

_____

_____

_____

Day 218

"CHARACTER AND INTEGRITY ARE VITAL."

Points to Ponder

In your own words, write a short summary of what Godly character and integrity mean to you. Spend some time meditating on what you write down.

_____

_____

_____

_____

_____

_____

Day 219

"ARE YOU BUILT TO CHANGE?"

Points to Ponder

If making changes is a requirement for you to become better, are you built to change? Are there areas of your life that are resistant to change? List them here and ask God to make you more open to adjustments.

_____

_____

_____

_____

_____

_____

Day 220

"CONVICTION SHOULD CARRY WEIGHT."

Points to Ponder

How do you feel when God convicts you of sin?

_____

_____

_____

_____

_____

_____

Day 221

"CHARACTER IS NOT WHAT
YOU DO WHEN PEOPLE ARE
WATCHING; IT'S WHAT YOU DO
WHEN PEOPLE ARE NOT
WATCHING YOU."

Points to Ponder

What does your life look like when people are not around you?

_____

_____

_____

_____

_____

_____

Vitamin D

DEVOTION TO GOD

Devotion to God

Nothing matches experiencing the pure, liberating presence of God. It is true that whoever desires God will live beyond the mundane and will experience Grace differently. Yes, Grace for forgiveness but even more Grace to live victoriously. This amazing Grace is evident in our devotion to and with God. Charles Haddon Spurgeon, the famous, English preacher once wrote, "I must take care above all that I cultivate communion with Christ, for though that can never be the basis of my peace - mark that - yet it will be the channel of it." This peace, as Dr Spurgeon alludes to, induces an equanimity of mind. This balanced place ensures that as we encounter the ebbs and flows of daily existence. We will handle it with dignity and strength. This results from quiet time with God. The incredible covenant one can have with God will as well cause you to love consistently and obey courageously.

Vitamin D, when digested, intentionally moves you into an unusual place of reflection. It is designed to enhance your spiritual growth by providing you with practical thoughts on love, loyalty, and enthusiasm. Each vitamin will grow your relationship with God and strengthen your devotion to God. You will wake up each day thirsting for the voice of God. It will open you up to the ever evolving possibilities embedded in intimacy with God. You will feel differently about your life and you will personally witness growth in your life of worship.

Day 222

"A SEASON OF SILENCE DOESN'T MEAN THAT GOD WON'T SPEAK EVENTUALLY."

Points to Ponder

If you happen to go through a season when God is silent, don't panic. Stay the course so that when He does speak you will be ready. How might you endure the silence?

_____

_____

_____

_____

_____

_____

Day 223

"JUST BECAUSE YOU HAVE ENEMIES DOESN'T MEAN YOU DO NOT HAVE FAVOR."

Points to Ponder

Read Luke 6: 27-30. Love your enemies so that God can continue to show you favor.

_____

_____

_____

_____

_____

_____

Day 224

"YOU CAN ALWAYS CONVICT
GOD OF BLESSINGS BECAUSE
EVIDENCE IS IN HIS NAME
(JESUS)."

Points to Ponder

Consistently call on Jesus Christ. The blessings are in His name! Name one thing that you are grateful for today.

_____

_____

_____

_____

_____

_____

Day 225

"JUST BECAUSE PEOPLE ARE
IN PLACE AND A PART OF THE
PROCESS DOESN'T MEAN THEY
WILL BE THERE FOR THE
OUTCOME."

Points to Ponder

As you navigate through life, remember that who may have been with you at the beginning may not necessarily be there at the end. Trust God and allow His love to funnel through you.

_____

_____

_____

_____

_____

_____

Day 226

"GOD WILL WORK YOU AROUND YOUR ENEMIES SO THEY DON'T DRAIN YOUR ENERGY OR YOUR ANOINTING."

Points to Ponder

Do you have people in your life who seem to be draining you? If you do, turn them over to God and allow Him to preserve your energy.

Day 227

"I DON'T NEED SOMEONE ELSE'S JOURNEY TO VALIDATE MY ANOINTING."

Points to Ponder

What is God showing you within your own journey that validates your anointing?

_____

_____

_____

_____

_____

_____

Day 228

"RELATIONSHIPS ARE NOT A STATEMENT OF YOUR INABILITY BUT A PARTNER IN YOUR POSSIBILITY."

Read Ecclesiastes 4:9-12.

Points to Ponder

Read Ecclesiastes 4:9-12 and summarize your thoughts.

_____

_____

_____

_____

_____

_____

Day 229

"STRESS IS DESIGNED BY THE ENEMY TO BREAK YOUR SPIRIT AND FOR YOU TO BECOME SOMEONE GOD NEVER DESIGNED YOU TO BECOME."

Read Philippians 4:6.

Points to Ponder

Read Philippians 4:6. Is every area of your life a reflection of God's love and grace? Which areas aren't? Purpose to be ALL that God has destined you to be TODAY.

_____

_____

_____

_____

_____

_____

Day 230

"MAKE THE PURITY OF YOUR INNER LIFE YOUR PRIORITY. A CLEAN HEART AND A GOOD NAME IS MORE VALUABLE THAN MONEY."

Read Proverbs 22:1.

Points to Ponder

Read Proverbs 22:1 and explain how a pure heart relates to having a good name.

_____

_____

_____

_____

_____

_____

Day 231

"MANY WANT THE PLATFORM OF THE PREACHER BUT NOT THE PAIN AND BURDEN OF THE PASTOR."

Points to Ponder

How can a desire for platforms more than the desire to go through the process affect your ability to influence others? How may it affect you personally?

_____

_____

_____

_____

_____

_____

Day 232

"THE PERSON WHO COMMITS TO THE CALL TO PREACH MUST FIRST COMMIT TO THE PROCESS OF PRAYER AND PREPARATION."

Points to Ponder

In your own words, explain why prayer and preparation are necessary for the assignment that God has given you.

_____

_____

_____

_____

_____

_____

Day 233

"IT'S AMAZING HOW ONE PERSON CAN **CHANGE** YOUR FORTUNES AND STATUS. THAT'S WHAT JESUS DID FOR US!"

Points to Ponder

Take some time to write down some of the AMAZING things that God has done for you that have changed the fortune of your life.

_____

_____

_____

_____

_____

_____

Day 234

"NEVER SAY **YES** IN THE NATURAL TO SOMETHING YOU HAVE NOT FIRST SOLD OUT TO IN THE **SPIRIT**."

Points to Ponder

Have you ever had an experience in which you agreed to do something but in your heart and your spirit you were hesitant to move forward? How will you prevent this in the future—making sure that you are at peace spiritually before you agree naturally?

_____

_____

_____

_____

_____

_____

Day 235

"PASTORS TRUST THE TIMING
OF GOD, NOT THE PROMISES
OF PEOPLE. THE NEXT GREAT
DOOR OF YOUR MINISTRY IS
NOT ON YOU—IT'S ON GOD."

Points to Ponder

Make the commitment to trust God with
opening the next great door in your life.

_____

_____

_____

_____

_____

_____

Day 236

"I PRAY GREAT VICTORY IN YOUR LIFE. I PRAY YOU EXPERIENCE THE ALIGNMENT IN YOUR RELATIONSHIPS THAT FRAMES UNITY WITH JESUS CHRIST."

Points to Ponder

If Jesus Christ represents unity, our relationships should also be unified. Take the time today to pray for a greater spirit of unity in your relationships and partnerships.

Day 237

"THE ENEMY'S JOB IS TO CONTAMINATE YOUR THINKING, TWISTING YOUR PERCEPTION OF THE PROCESS THAT'S ORDAINED FOR YOU TO BECOME GREAT."

Points to Ponder

In what ways has the enemy tried to deceive you into thinking that your process was your ending? Today, pray to God and thank Him for the process He has given you for the purpose of your development.

_____

_____

_____

_____

_____

_____

Day 238

"SPIRITUAL MATURITY IS THE ABILITY TO STAY THE COURSE OF YOUR ASSIGNMENT EVEN WHILE DEALING WITH PERSONAL PAIN AND DISAPPOINTMENT."

Points to Ponder

What personal pain or disappointments are you dealing with right now? How are you making the commitment to stay on the course that God has for you despite what you are going through?

_____

_____

_____

_____

_____

_____

Day 239

"GOD HONORS RESILIENCY."

Points to Ponder

Define resiliency and explain how you have had to exemplify it in your personal journey with God.

_____

_____

_____

_____

_____

_____

Day 240

"PASTORING IS SUCH A UNIQUE ASSIGNMENT. MANY WANT TO DO IT BUT FEW REALLY GET IT. IT'S ABOUT PEOPLE NOT BUILDINGS, BUDGETS OR BYLAWS. IT'S ABOUT LOVING THE PEOPLE. I LOVE THIS CALL EVEN WITH ITS CHALLENGES."

Points to Ponder

In the unique assignment that God has called you to, are you embracing the challenges that come with it?

_____

_____

_____

_____

_____

_____

Day 241

"SLAVES OBEY JESUS OUT OF
OBLIGATION AND A SENSE OF
DRUDGERY. A FRIEND OBEYS OUT
OF LOVE AND AND JOY. STRIVE TO
DEVELOP A RELATIONSHIP OF
LOVE AND INTIMACY WITH JESUS
AND YOUR ATTITUDE TOWARDS HIM
WILL BE MUCH BETTER. LOVE
LOVING HIM AND ENJOY OBEYING
HIM."

Points to Ponder

How can you ensure that you are developing a
"friendship" with Jesus Christ?

_____

_____

_____

_____

_____

_____

Day 242

"THE PURITY OF YOUR RELATIONSHIP WITH GOD IS ABOUT THE TRUTH OF YOUR HEART."

Points to Ponder

Read Psalm 139:23 and make a commitment to spending quality time with God.

_____

_____

_____

_____

_____

_____

Day 243

"WE MUST GET OUT OF GOD'S WAY BUT STAY IN HIS FACE."

Points to Ponder

Make a consistent commitment to staying in God's presence through prayer while allowing Him to lead the way.

_____

_____

_____

_____

_____

_____

Day 244

"FATHER CLEANSE OUR
HEARTS OF ANYTHING THAT
MISDIRECTS OUR FOCUS,
CAUSES US TO MISMANAGE
OUR ASSIGNMENT, OR
INDUCES US TO MISUSE OUR
WORDS."

Points to Ponder

How can you ensure that the primary focus of
your heart on the assignment that God has
given you?

_____

_____

_____

_____

_____

_____

Day 245

"I ONCE HEARD A POWERFUL
STATEMENT. 'WE MIGHT AS
WELL BE TOGETHER BECAUSE
THE DEVIL SEES US ALL AS
HIS ENEMY.'"

Points to Ponder

Who is a part of your life right now that you
can form a greater alliance with? How can they
contribute to deepening your spiritual walk?

_____

_____

_____

_____

_____

_____

Day 246

"DEVELOP A **PRAYER LIFE**
AND NOT JUST MOMENTS
WHEN YOU PRAY. YOUR
CONSISTENCY WILL PRODUCE
THE GODLY RESPONSE YOU
DESIRE."

Points to Ponder

Commit yourself to a consistent prayer life. Describe your prayer life and indicate any areas for improvement.

_____

_____

_____

_____

_____

_____

Day 247

"IN THIS SEASON, YOUR CHOICE OF PRAYER PARTNERS WILL BE AS IMPORTANT AS YOUR CHOICE OF FRIENDS. DISCERN WHO CAN WALK WITH YOU IN THIS SEASON IN PRAYER. THEIR FAITH AND ENERGY MUST MATCH YOURS."

Points to Ponder

Identify a person or people around you who can partner with you in prayer. What qualifies them to partner with you?

_____

_____

_____

_____

_____

_____

Day 248

"LOVING YOUR ENEMIES IS
MORE THAN JUST TOLERATING
THEM. IT'S ULTIMATELY ABOUT
WANTING THE BEST FOR
THEM."

Read Jeremiah 29:7.

Points to Ponder

How can you handle situations of adversity at
the hands of others so you are still able to
desire the best for them while demonstrating
the character of God?

_____

_____

_____

_____

_____

_____

Day 249

"GOD HAS POSITIONED YOU SO
THAT THE ONLY PERSON WHO
CAN STOP YOUR BLESSING IS
YOU. PLEASE GET OUT OF
YOUR WAY!"

Points to Ponder

Make an effort to totally trust God with your future. Describe the area(s) of your life that you have refused to completely submit to God—believing that you can do it alone. Give them to God today!

_____

_____

_____

_____

_____

_____

Day 250

"FAMILIES WHO STRUGGLE
DON'T KNOW HOW TO
CONFRONT THEIR DEEP-
SEEDED ISSUES. WHEN
ISSUES GO UNADDRESSED,
THEY HAUNT GENERATION
AFTER GENERATION."

Points to Ponder

Have you ever identified a struggle within your family that has gone unaddressed? What will you do to address it so that it doesn't affect your next generation?

_____

_____

_____

_____

_____

_____

Day 251

"THE ENEMY HAS TRICKED
MANY OF US INTO SETTLING
FOR WHAT WE HATE BECAUSE
WE ARE NOT WILLING TO
CHANGE TO GET WHAT WE
LOVE."

Points to Ponder

Reflect on what you desire but have yet to
receive. In what ways are you willing to make
positive changes to receive what God desires
for you to have?

_____

_____

_____

_____

_____

_____

Day 252

"THE REASON THE WARFARE
IS SO INTENSE FOR SOME OF
US IS BECAUSE WE ARE
DEALING WITH THE DEMONS
OF PEOPLE WE'VE NEVER
EVEN MET."

Points to Ponder

Take time today to identify some of the issues
you may have faced in life that seem to be
generational. Pray and ask God to give you the
wisdom to overcome them.

_____

_____

_____

_____

_____

_____

Day 253

"MY CHILDREN WILL GET THE GOD I GIVE THEM. WE MUST MAKE GOD OBVIOUS."

Points to Ponder

What are you doing to consistently keep the presence and the example of Jesus Christ in front of your children? How will you make sure that His presence is a consistent part of their development?

_____

_____

_____

_____

_____

_____

Day 254

"HUMILITY ALLOWS ME TO SWALLOW YOU WITHOUT VOMITING MY BLESSING."

Points to Ponder

Has God placed anyone in your life that is testing your humility based on how they are treating you? How will you continue to manage them to ensure that you remain humble?

_____

_____

_____

_____

_____

_____

Day 255

"THE PURPOSE OF A WAR ROOM IS TO PREPARE YOU FOR VICTORY."

Points to Ponder

Describe the personal space that you use to pray. How have you consecrated this space for time with God?

_____

_____

_____

_____

_____

_____

Day 256

"WHY OPEN YOUR MOUTH TO
PRAY IF YOU DON'T EXPECT
ANYTHING TO CHANGE."

Points to Ponder

Are you praying with expectation that God will change the situation you are praying about? Write down what you are expecting God to do through your prayers.

_____

_____

_____

_____

_____

_____

Day 257

"PRAYER DOES NOT HAPPEN
IN AN IMPURE HEART."

Points to Ponder

How can you ensure that your heart is pure
before seeking God in prayer.

_____

_____

_____

_____

_____

_____

Day 258

"HESITATION WILL CAUSE YOU TO MISS THE TIMING GOD."

Points to Ponder

Is God telling you to make a move that you are hesitant about? Describe it here.

_____

_____

_____

_____

_____

_____

Day 259

"YOU CAN'T LET YOUR MOOD BE YOUR MOMENT."

Points to Ponder

When you have a bad moment, don't allow it to shape your attitude. Press your way through.

_____

_____

_____

_____

_____

_____

Day 260

"YOU CAN BE **BIG** WITH
LITTLE WHEN YOU HAVE
WISDOM; AND YOU CAN BE
SMALL WITH PLENTY WITHOUT
WISDOM."

Points to Ponder

Today ask God for wisdom, knowledge, and understanding. Read Proverbs 4:6-7.

_____

_____

_____

_____

_____

_____

Day 261

"YOUR GREATEST VICTORY IS
WHEN YOU CAN BLESS YOUR
ENEMIES AS AN INDICATOR OF
YOUR MATURITY."

Points to Ponder

In what ways can you bless those who have
caused or are causing there to be friction in
your life?

_____

_____

_____

_____

_____

Day 262

"Never let jealousy consume you, especially when God trusts you with exposure."

Points to Ponder

What are you doing to overcome the spirit of jealousy if it exists within you?

_____

_____

_____

_____

_____

_____

Day 263

"THE GOAL OF THE ENEMY IS
TO CAUSE YOU TO ADJUST TO
HIM THROUGH INCREMENTAL
DECISIONS."

Points to Ponder

How are your short term decisions impacting God's long term plans for your life? Ask God to strengthen your faith to continue trusting His plan.

_____

_____

_____

_____

_____

_____

Day 264

"THE GLORY DOESN'T COME WHERE YOU'RE WANTED; IT COMES WHERE YOU'RE NEEDED."

Points to Ponder

Where does God need you to be in this season for His glory to manifest?

_____

_____

_____

_____

_____

_____

Day 265

"THE PURITY OF YOUR HEART
WILL ALWAYS OVERCOME THE
MISTAKES OF YOUR HAND."

Points to Ponder

In what ways has the purity of your heart
allowed you to overcome mistakes and given
you favor with God?

_____

_____

_____

_____

_____

_____

Day 266

"SOMETIMES A MISTAKE IS
THE REVELATION OF YOUR
POSSIBILITY."

Points to Ponder

How have your mistakes encouraged you to
never give up?

_____

_____

_____

_____

_____

Day 267

"IF YOU HAVE FOOD IN YOUR BELLY BUT NO PEACE IN YOUR SPIRIT, YOU'RE STILL HUNGRY."

Points to Ponder

Commit to consistently feeding yourself with the Word of God.

_____

_____

_____

_____

_____

_____

Day 268

"UNITY DOES NOT MEAN THAT WE DON'T HAVE CONFLICT."

Points to Ponder

Read 1 Peter 3:8 and make a commitment to be compassionate and humble even when you face a conflict.

_____

_____

_____

_____

_____

_____

Day 269

"GOD GIVES YOU IDEAS IN ORDER TO PUSH YOU TO NEW LEVELS."

Points to Ponder

Write down any ideas God has given you and pray for a strategy on how to carry them out.

_____

_____

_____

_____

_____

_____

Day 270

"THE BEST WAY TO KILL
FOOLISHNESS AND NEGATIVITY IS TO
FACE IT AND EXPOSE IT. GOD
HONORS THE HUMBLE AND WILL
GRANT HIS PEACE WHEN YOU
MANAGE IT IN A WAY THAT CLEARLY
COMMUNICATES THAT. MOVE ON AND
WATCH GOD."

Points to Ponder

Make a list of the foolish and negative things
you know God is calling you to cut out of your
life. Once you complete the list, declare that
each area is in the past and will no longer
consume you.

Day 271

"FOLKS DON'T KNOW YOUR STORY, SO THEY DON'T KNOW YOUR STRENGTH."

Points to Ponder

Who can you encourage with your story? Identify at least one person that you will share your personal testimony with so that they can be inspired to live a greater life for Jesus Christ.

_____

_____

_____

_____

_____

_____

Day 272

"NURTURE GETS YOU READY AND POSITIONS YOU."

Points to Ponder

If you have someone who is committed to nurturing you throughout your process, embrace it so that you will be prepared for positioning.

_____

_____

_____

_____

_____

_____

Day 273

"YOU'RE DRIPPING WITH AUTHORITY."

Points to Ponder

Read Luke 10:19 and summarize how it applies to you as a child of God.

_____

_____

_____

_____

_____

_____

Day 274

"STOP STRUGGLING IN EVERY RELATIONSHIP."

Points to Ponder

In what way(s) do you struggle in your relationship with others? What sacrifices are you willing to make to struggle less?

_____

_____

_____

_____

_____

_____

Day 275

"EMBRACE THE REALITY OF THE REJECTION."

Points to Ponder

If you happen to experience rejection of any kind, face it so that you can move forward peacefully. Reflect on your past and identify something positive that resulted from rejection.

_____

_____

_____

_____

_____

_____

Day 276

"GOD PUTS YOU IN FAMINE AND ADVERSITY TO MAKE YOUR CIRCLE SMALLER."

Points to Ponder

Write down examples of times when you faced adversity and it forced you to rely on God more than the people around you.

_____

_____

_____

_____

_____

_____

Day 277

"EVERY LEVEL OF PROMOTION AND ELEVATION REQUIRES NURTURERS."

Points to Ponder

As you make progress in life, place a high value on the person that God places in your life to nurture you.

Day 278

"ADVERSITY EXPOSES YOUR MATURITY."

Points to Ponder

Can you recall a time in which the adversity you faced in a situation exposed your maturity level? How did you grow from the experience?

_____

_____

_____

_____

_____

_____

Day 279

"WHO HAS GROWN WITH YOU—WHO HAS GOD INSERTED TO MATCH YOUR ELEVATION?"

Points to Ponder

Today, take some time to identify one person God has allowed to grow with you and one person that God has inserted to be an asset to where He is taking you.

_____

_____

_____

_____

_____

_____

Day 280

"DO THE PEOPLE IN YOUR CIRCLE CARRY WEIGHT TO PUSH YOU OR ARE THEY WEIGHTY?"

Points to Ponder

Take the time to assess the people in your circle and determine whether they are pushing you or simply pulling you down.

_____

_____

_____

_____

_____

_____

Day 281

"DON'T BE AFRAID TO ADD ADVISERS."

Points to Ponder

Who is God placing around you that can serve as a positive adviser? Are you open to receiving their advice?

_____

_____

_____

_____

_____

_____

Day 282

"DAVID CONSTRUCTED HIS LIFE ON NON-NEGOTIABLE CONVICTION."

Points to Ponder

Are your convictions concerning God non-negotiable? How can they become even stronger?

_____

_____

_____

_____

_____

_____

Day 283

"LOYALTY ISN'T JUST A WORK—IT'S A LIFESTYLE.

Points to Ponder

What and who has your loyalty in this season? Are those things a healthy reflection of a lifestyle that honors God?

_____

_____

_____

_____

_____

_____

Day 284

"IF YOU CAN LEARN FROM IT, YOU CAN BUILD ON IT."

Points to Ponder

What have you experienced in life that you have committed to learning from? Do you make the consistent effort to allow every experience to become a learning experience?

Day 285

"EXPERIENCE IS BETTER THAN CREDIT."

Points to Ponder

How have your experiences helped you to make better quality decisions as you have progressed in life?

_____

_____

_____

_____

_____

_____

Day 286

"WHEN YOU'RE GOING
THROUGH LEADERSHIP
DEVELOPMENT, IT'S NOT JUST
A CLASS, IT'S A
RELATIONSHIP."

Points to Ponder

Write down the name of the primary leader in your life and explain how God is developing your leadership skills through your relationship with them.

_____

_____

_____

_____

_____

_____

Day 287

"RECEIVE FROM NURTURERS WITHOUT GIVING YOUR OPINION."

Points to Ponder

When you receive correction, are you quick to give your opinion or do you simply receive?

_____

_____

_____

_____

_____

_____

Day 288

"YOUR ANOINTING BECOMES DAMAGED WHEN YOU CAN'T HANDLE NURTURE."

Points to Ponder

What adjustments can you make to handle nurturing better? Are you willing to make these adjustments for the sake of preserving your anointing?

_____

_____

_____

_____

_____

_____

Day 289

"NURTURE IS A PROCESS."

Points to Ponder

Write down one scenario in which you were nurtured and explain the process that you experienced.

_____

_____

_____

_____

_____

_____

Day 290

"YOUR GIFT ONLY GETS YOU IDENTIFIED. IT DOESN'T GET YOU PROMOTED."

Points to Ponder

Make a commitment to allow the gifts that God has given you to be nurtured, so that you will be ready for promotion.

_____

_____

_____

_____

_____

_____

Day 291

"YOU WILL NEVER REACH
YOUR GREATEST LEVEL IF
YOU'RE NOT NURTURED."

Points to Ponder

If someone is assigned to nurture you, let them.
Reaching your full potential depends on it.

_____

_____

_____

_____

_____

_____

Vitamin E

EXTRAORDINARY
LIVING FOR GOD

Extraordinary Living for God

Do you know who you are? Do you have any clue what God has created you to be? Imagine if you could come to this amazing revelation regarding your God ordained purpose and potential. What would be the quality of your life? In essence, imagine if you knew how extraordinary you are—what a life you would experience!

Understand that living extraordinary is not only desired but very possible. God has, through Jesus Christ, given you the resources inwardly and outwardly to be great beyond your wildest imagination. Being extraordinary is about being fulfilled, successful and abundant. It is about transcending limits and rising above narrowing thoughts that seek to confine us. In essence, it's God's will that we live as conquerors—overcoming through Jesus Christ.

Vitamin E is designed to press and push you to live an extraordinary life for Jesus Christ. When digested, each thought will inspire, motivate and energize you to be your best you. You will believe that God has so much for you and you will not settle for anything less than what you discern as your God-ordained purpose. You will love, laugh, give and produce beyond your wildest imagination. And what's so exciting is that this is God's will for you. So enjoy the journey and watch God do the extraordinary in and through you.

Day 292

"WE ARE THE LETTERS OF RECOMMENDATION FOR JESUS CHRIST."

Read 2 Corinthians 3:2.

Points to Ponder

In what ways does your life positively and effectively represent Christ? In what ways does it require improvement?

_____

_____

_____

_____

_____

_____

Day 293

"YOUR LIFE NEEDS TO BE A REFLECTION OF THE GLORY OF GOD."

Points to Ponder

Read Psalm 24. How can your life be a greater reflection of God's glory?

_____

_____

_____

_____

_____

_____

Day 294

"THE BEST WAY TO SHUT UP A
CRITIC IS TO SHOW EVIDENCE
OF GOD'S FAVOR AND
PRESENCE IN YOUR LIFE.
THEY CAN'T DENY WHAT THEY
SEE."

Read 1 Samuel 18:28.

Points to Ponder

How can you better allow your life—saturated
with God's grace and favor—to speak for you
as opposed to justifying it for critics?

_____

_____

_____

_____

_____

_____

Day 295

"LET YOUR CRITICS KEEP
FOLLOWING YOU. THEY WILL
EVENTUALLY GET TRAPPED IN
THE MIRACLE OF GOD'S GRACE
IN YOUR LIFE."

Points to Ponder

Decide to not allow your critics to be a distraction. Stay on the course that God has designed for you.

_____

_____

_____

_____

_____

_____

Day 296

"THEY CAN CHANGE YOUR NAME BUT THEY SHOULD NEVER BE ABLE TO CHANGE YOUR CHARACTER."

Points to Ponder

No matter what people say about you or no matter what they call you, strive to demonstrate Godly character.

_____

_____

_____

_____

_____

_____

Day 297

"THEY CAN'T FINISH THE PUZZLE BECAUSE YOU ARE THE MISSING PIECE."

Read 1 Samuel 16:11-13.

Points to Ponder

Ask God to reveal opportunities for you to contribute to or become an asset to a person, project, or organization and trust that God will orchestrate each of your steps.

_____

_____

_____

_____

_____

_____

Day 298

"YOU CAN'T PRODUCE WHAT
YOU ARE CREATED TO
PRODUCE UNTIL YOU ARE
AUTHENTICALLY WHO GOD
CREATED YOU TO BE."

Points to Ponder

As God continues to make you who He
designed you to be, remain committed to the
process so that you can ultimately be an
authentic producer.

_____

_____

_____

_____

_____

_____

Day 299

"GOD IS ABOUT TO SHINE HIS LIGHT BASED ON THE ATTRACTIVENESS OF YOUR CHARACTER."

Points to Ponder

How can your character improve so that God's light can shine at the greatest level? Write down some traits that can be improved and declare that they will!.

_____

_____

_____

_____

_____

_____

Day 300

"YOU CAN'T BE AN EAGLE HANGING OUT WITH PIGEONS."

Read Isaiah 40:31.

Points to Ponder

Read Isaiah 40:31 and summarize how the scripture applies to your life.

_____

_____

_____

_____

_____

_____

Day 301

"YOUR HUMILITY PROTECTS YOU IN YOUR ELEVATION."

Points to Ponder

Make a commitment to consistent, Godly humility so that your promotion can be protected and preserved.

_____

_____

_____

_____

_____

_____

Day 302

"YOU CAN'T BECOME A *NEW* SOMETHING AND STAY THE *OLD* YOU."

Points to Ponder

What do you need God to "make new" in you so that you don't become delayed in the old?

_____

_____

_____

_____

_____

_____

Day 303

"BE DETERMINED TO SPEAK YOUR DESTINY—NOT YOUR DILEMMA."

Points to Ponder

Today commit to making positive declarations concerning your destiny. Allow your dilemma to die by NOT talking about it.

_____

_____

_____

_____

_____

_____

Day 304

"DON'T GET STUCK WHERE
GOD ORDERS YOUR PROCESS
OF REINVENTION TO BEGIN
AND MISS WHAT HE HAS FOR
YOU AT THE END."

Points to Ponder

Identify where God desires for your reinvention to begin and make the necessary moves as He leads you.

Day 305

"ADJUST TO YOUR NEW
SEASON! DON'T ALLOW
ANYONE TO DISCOURAGE YOU
FROM SHIFTING AND
CONFORMING TO WHAT COMES
WITH GOD'S REPOSITIONING
YOU."

Points to Ponder

Has God shifted your season? If He has, have
you made the proper adjustments to move with
Him?

_____

_____

_____

_____

_____

_____

Day 306

"IF YOU ARE DETERMINED TO LIVE THE BALANCE OF YOUR DAYS HONORING GOD THROUGH SERVICE TO OTHERS AND LIVING ACCOUNTABLE TO HIS STANDARD, SAY 'AMEN!'"

Points to Ponder

Read Colossians 3:23-24 and declare that your service is honorable to God and that your reward is in His promise.

_____

_____

_____

_____

_____

_____

Day 307

"THERE SHOULD COME A
SEASON IN YOUR LIFE WHEN
YOU HAVE MATURED TO SUCH
A PLACE THAT SMALL MINDED,
NEGATIVE, ATTENTION-
NEEDING PEOPLE CAN'T
POSSIBLY RESIDE IN YOUR
SPACE."

Points to Ponder

Ask God to make you so spiritually mature that you no longer give time or attention to negative people.

_____

_____

_____

_____

_____

_____

Day 308

"Do who you be.
Authenticity is the
pathway to God-ordained
success."

Points to Ponder

Does your spirituality and relationship with God reflect in your actions? If not, how can you align the two so that you can have God-ordained success?

_____

_____

_____

_____

_____

_____

Day 309

"MAY WE BE A HEALTHY
REFLECTION OF JESUS CHRIST
TO THOSE WHO ARE LOST AND
DESPERATELY NEED A
RELATIONSHIP WITH HIM."

Points to Ponder

When other people look at the example that
your life sets, are they inspired to develop a
relationship with Jesus Christ?

_____

_____

_____

_____

_____

_____

Day 310

"GOD HAS GIVEN YOU
EVERYTHING YOU NEED TO BE
EVERYTHING HE HAS
DESTINED YOU TO BE. NOW
IT'S TIME TO GIVE HIM ALL OF
YOU."

Points to Ponder

What can you give less time to in order to give
God more of you?

_____

_____

_____

_____

_____

_____

Day 311

"LIKE FLOUR IS NECESSARY
FOR A CAKE, CHARACTER IS
NECESSARY FOR GREATNESS."

Points to Ponder

Make the commitment to allow God to develop your character so that you can become great.

_____

_____

_____

_____

_____

_____

Day 312

"EMBRACE THE PROCESS AND ENJOY THE SPOILS."

Points to Ponder

Have you genuinely committed to embracing your process? Take some time and ask God to make you open to where He is taking you and how He will get you there.

_____

_____

_____

_____

_____

_____

Day 313

"MARRY OBEDIENCE WITH CREATIVITY AND WATCH GOD EXPAND YOU BEYOND YOUR WILDEST DREAMS."

Points to Ponder

What creative ideas has God given you that you can connect to obedience? Write down the ideas and start seeking Him right away!

_____

_____

_____

_____

_____

_____

Day 314

"YOUR GREATEST SEASON IS TIED TO YOUR WILLFUL COMMITMENT TO MAXIMIZE EACH AND EVERY DAY."

Points to Ponder

Seek to maximize each and every day so that you will always have the opportunity to live in your greatest season.

_____

_____

_____

_____

_____

_____

Day 315

"TODAY, **PRAY** FOR SOMEONE. **LAUGH** WITH SOMEONE. **SOW** INTO SOMEONE. **LOVE** SOMEONE. **SMILE** AT SOMEONE. AND **BLESS** SOMEONE!"

Points to Ponder

Today, make generosity a priority with everyone you come into contact with.

_____

_____

_____

_____

_____

_____

Day 316

"LIVE IN **EXPECTATION** BY DECLARING THE SEASON YOU DESIRE AND NOT THE SITUATION YOU PRESENTLY RESIDE IN."

Points to Ponder

Live EXPECTING the very best, no matter what situation you may face. Create a vision for your next season and describe it.

_____

_____

_____

_____

_____

_____

Day 317

"KNOW THE POWER OF YOUR
WORDS AND USE THEM WITH
INTENT AND PURPOSE."

Read Proverbs 18:21.

Points to Ponder

How can you better refrain from speaking
negatively or using words to harm others?

_____

_____

_____

_____

_____

_____

Day 318

"BEING HEALTHY AND HOLY IS A CHOICE. CHOOSE TO BE HEALTHY AND HOLY. THE BENEFITS OF JOY, PEACE, AND PROSPERITY WILL BLOW YOU AWAY!"

Points to Ponder

Is your life built for you to not only live healthy and holy, but to also experience the benefits of a holy and healthy life?

_____

_____

_____

_____

_____

_____

Day 319

"YOU WERE BORN A WINNER, SO GO WIN IN JESUS NAME!"

Points to Ponder

Write down the statement, "I'm a winner!" and declare it over and over again.

_____

_____

_____

_____

_____

_____

Day 320

"WE MUST CULTIVATE A SERVANT SPIRIT IN OUR HOMES."

Points to Ponder

Does your family view you as a servant? How can you demonstrate the spirit of servant-hood on a greater level in your family?

_____

_____

_____

_____

_____

_____

Day 321

"MY DESTINY IS NOT IN *YOUR* HANDS. IT'S IN GOD'S HANDS."

Points to Ponder

Read Psalm 25: 1-3 and write a brief reflection.

_____

_____

_____

_____

_____

_____

Day 322

"REINVENTION IS A REQUIREMENT FOR GREATNESS."

Points to Ponder

Are you willing to go through the process of reinvention so that God can prepare you for greatness?

_____

_____

_____

_____

_____

Day 323

"NO MATTER WHAT YOU MAY
EXPERIENCE, DON'T EVER
BECOME A PRISONER TO
DISAPPOINTMENT."

Points to Ponder

Can you recall a time that you experienced
disappointment? How did you handle it so that
it didn't hold you captive?

_____

_____

_____

_____

_____

_____

Day 324

"EXTRAORDINARY PEOPLE FIND THE LEAK IN THEIR GENERATION."

Points to Ponder

What has God exposed you to in your generation that He wants you to assist in resolving?

_____

_____

_____

_____

_____

_____

Day 325

"THIS IS A SEASON WHERE
YOU WILL WALK INTO A ROOM
AND YOUR EXCELLENCE WILL
CAUSE YOU TO HAVE
ENEMIES."

Points to Ponder

Are you committed to being excellent at the
expense of having enemies?

_____

_____

_____

_____

_____

_____

Day 326

"EXTRAORDINARY PEOPLE THRIVE ON OPPORTUNITY."

Points to Ponder

What opportunities has God given you that should have caused you to thrive?

_____

_____

_____

_____

_____

_____

Day 327

"BE EXCELLENT EVERYWHERE SO YOU CAN BE TRUSTED ANYWHERE."

Points to Ponder

Read Daniel 6:9. Make a commitment to strive for excellence in ALL that you do, so that God can trust you wherever He sends you.

_____

_____

_____

_____

_____

_____

Day 328

"EVEN WHEN THEY DON'T
MENTION YOUR NAME, YOU
SHOULD STILL HAVE AN
IMPACT."

Points to Ponder

Strive to be so excellent at what you do that your impact isn't determined by the acknowledgement of other people.

_____

_____

_____

_____

_____

_____

Day 329

"WHEN CONFESSION AND BELIEF LINE UP, SUCCESS AND VICTORY WILL FOLLOW."

Points to Ponder

Are your confession and belief levels as high as they can be? How can your time of confessing and your faith be improved?

_____

_____

_____

_____

_____

_____

Day 330

"YOU MAY EXPERIENCE FAILURES IN LIFE, BUT YOU CAN STILL LIVE EXTRAORDINARY."

Points to Ponder

Learn from your failures so that you can live extraordinary as you move forward.

_____

_____

_____

_____

_____

_____

Day 331

"EXTRAORDINARY PEOPLE
DON'T MISS MOMENTS OF
ASSIGNMENT."

Points to Ponder

Have you ever missed a moment of God's assignment? How did you handle it? What have you done recently to make sure that you don't miss an assignment in the future?

_____

_____

_____

_____

_____

_____

Day 332

"AN EXTRAORDINARY LIFE IS A LIFE THAT CONTINUES TO LEARN."

Points to Ponder

What is God allowing to happen in your life right now that is designed to teach you something? Write it down and summarize what you are learning.

_____

_____

_____

_____

_____

_____

Day 333

"THERE'S A DIFFERENCE BETWEEN BEING NOTABLE AND NOTEWORTHY."

Points to Ponder

In your own words, write the difference between "notable" and "noteworthy." How can God be glorified once we become "notable."

_____

_____

_____

_____

_____

_____

Day 334

"WHEN YOU REINVENT YOURSELF, YOU ALLOW GOD TO OPEN THE FLOODGATES."

Points to Ponder

How does reinvention apply to you personally? If reinvention allows God to give you unlimited opportunities, is the process of reinvention worth going through?

_____

_____

_____

_____

_____

Day 335

"THE FRUSTRATION OF GOD IS
THAT HE SELECTS US TO BE
EXTRAORDINARY AND WE
SETTLE FOR AVERAGE."

Points to Ponder

Make a consistent commitment to strive for
the level of fulfillment that God desires for you
to have in every area of your life. Believe that
you can live EXTRAORDINARY!

_____

_____

_____

_____

_____

_____

Day 336

"WHEN YOU CENTER YOUR
IDENTITY AROUND JESUS
CHRIST, YOU HAVE NO NEED
TO COMPETE WITH ANYONE.
YOU UNDERSTAND THE
UNIQUE PURPOSE OF YOUR
ASSIGNMENT."

Points to Ponder

Have you taken the necessary time to seek God concerning the unique assignment that He has given you? Today spend time with Him and write down what He shows you.

Day 337

"DON'T BE SO EASILY
OFFENDED WHEN PEOPLE
DON'T LIKE YOU OR DESPISE
YOU. THEY ARE TEACHING YOU
HOW TO LOVE YOURSELF."

Points to Ponder

Can you recall a time when someone rejected
you? How did you respond to the rejection?
How have you matured so that rejection will
cause you to love yourself more?

_____

_____

_____

_____

_____

_____

Day 338

"ONE OF THE WORST THINGS YOU CAN DO IS ACT LIKE THEY DIDN'T HURT YOU WHEN THEY ACTUALLY DID. EMBRACE THE PAIN, BUT DON'T GIVE THE PAIN PERMISSION TO BLOCK YOUR PROMOTION."

Points to Ponder

Are you allowing pain that you have experienced in the past to hinder you from enjoying the promotion that God has for you in this season?

_____

_____

_____

_____

_____

_____

Day 339

"GOD ISN'T BUILDING YOU TO
SURVIVE; HE'S BUILDING YOU
TO THRIVE!"

Points to Ponder

What adjustments can you make spiritually and
physically to ensure that you are not simply
surviving? Have you defined your long term
goals? Write them down and declare that you
will THRIVE!

_____

_____

_____

_____

_____

_____

Day 340

"EXCELLENCE IS GIVING YOUR
VERY BEST EVERY TIME YOU
GET THE PRIVILEGE TO
SERVE."

Points to Ponder

When you serve, do you ALWAYS give your
very best? Read Colossians 3:17 and write a
brief reflection.

_____

_____

_____

_____

_____

_____

Day 341

"FOCUS ON THE PRIZE, NOT THE PROCESS."

Read Philippians 3:10-14.

Points to Ponder

Do your very best to focus on your goals and dreams rather than focusing on how challenging it may be to achieve them.

_____

_____

_____

_____

_____

_____

Day 342

"WHEN YOU ARE IN AN 'ONLY GOD CAN' SEASON, YOU ARE IN THE RIGHT PLACE."

Read Habakkuk 3:17-19.

Points to Ponder

Read Habakkuk 3:17-19 and summarize your thoughts.

_____

_____

_____

_____

_____

_____

Day 343

"WHEN GOD PUTS YOU BACK
TOGETHER, HE WILL COVER
YOU."

Points to Ponder

Identify a time when God put things back
together in your life. What did you discover
about the covering of God when you went
through the experience?

_____

_____

_____

_____

_____

_____

Day 344

"NO MORE INDECISION! STAGNATION AND THE UNWILLINGNESS TO MOVE FORWARD WILL NO LONGER HOLD UP THINGS—IT WILL CANCEL THEM."

Points to Ponder

What is God calling you to move forward with that you have been delaying? Write it down and declare that you are "Moving Forward."

_____

_____

_____

_____

_____

_____

Day 345

"YOU CAN MISS A WHOLE NEW SEASON BECAUSE YOU REFUSE TO MAKE A DECISION AND MOVE FORWARD. GOD SAYS, 'MOVE FORWARD!'"

Points to Ponder

Today, obey God and move forward!

_____

_____

_____

_____

_____

_____

Day 346

"When you're special and unique, you can't hang with everybody."

Points to Ponder

Is there anyone in your circle from whom God is calling you to separate?

_____

_____

_____

_____

_____

Day 347

"YOUR ACTIVITY IS AFFECTED BY YOUR ATTITUDE."

Points to Ponder

How has your attitude affected your activity? What can you do to make sure that your attitude is as positive as possible?

Day 348

"WHEN YOU'RE A POSITIVE REFLECTION, PEOPLE FOLLOW."

Points to Ponder

Make a commitment to being a positive reflection of Jesus Christ. Read Matthew 5:13 and note your thoughts.

_____

_____

_____

_____

_____

_____

Day 349

"EXTRAORDINARY PEOPLE KEEP THEIR WORD."

Points to Ponder

Read Ecclesiastes 5:4-7. Strive to always keep your word so that you can live an extraordinary life.

_____

_____

_____

_____

_____

_____

Day 350

"DON'T ALLOW PEOPLE IN
YOUR LIFE WITHOUT AN
EXPECTATION OF
EXCELLENCE."

Points to Ponder

Raise the standards of the people around you so that you will be challenged to live extraordinary.

_____

_____

_____

_____

_____

_____

Day 351

"EXTRAORDINARY PEOPLE LIVE BY HIGH STANDARDS."

Points to Ponder

Are your standards at the level that God expects them to be? In what way(s) can you raise the standards in your own life?

_____

_____

_____

_____

_____

_____

Day 352

"DOES YOUR LIFE INSPIRE ANYBODY TO BE BETTER?"

Points to Ponder

Who is God using your life to impact? Write down the name of one person that is influenced by your life and pray for them.

_____

_____

_____

_____

_____

_____

Day 353

"LEAVING A LEGACY IS THE RESULT OF EXTRAORDINARY LIVING."

Points to Ponder

Write down the type of legacy you want to leave behind for your seed to inherit.

_____

_____

_____

_____

_____

_____

Day 354

"ELEVATION COMES WITH ACCOUNTABILITY AND RESPONSIBILITY."

Points to Ponder

Can you better handle the level of accountability and responsibility that comes with elevation?

_____

_____

_____

_____

_____

_____

Day 355

"EXTRAORDINARY PEOPLE DON'T CUT DEALS."

Points to Ponder

What do you do when you are tempted to take shortcuts to accomplish your goals? How will you resist the temptation to cut deals?

_____

_____

_____

_____

_____

_____

Day 356

"EXTRAORDINARY PEOPLE UNDERSTAND LOYALTY."

Points to Ponder

Write down what the word "loyalty" means to you. How does loyalty relate to your personal relationship with Jesus Christ?

_____

_____

_____

_____

_____

_____

Day 357

"STOP BEING YOUR POSITION AND NOT YOUR IDENTITY."

Points to Ponder

Have you allowed your position to define your identity? Commit to making your identity a priority rather than your position.

_____

_____

_____

_____

_____

_____

Day 358

"EVERYBODY HAS POTENTIAL.
IT'S DURING PREPARATION
THAT YOUR IDENTITY IS
DISCOVERED."

Points to Ponder

How is God using your preparation period to reveal your identity?

_____

_____

_____

_____

_____

_____

Day 359

"LIVING EXTRAORDINARY
LIVES MARRIES GODLY
CHARACTER AND EXCELLENT
CONDUCT."

Points to Ponder

In what ways can your character and your conduct improve? Write down some of the areas in which you want God to intervene.

Day 360

"YOUR ATTITUDE DETERMINES YOUR OUTCOME."

Points to Ponder

Take the time today to assess your attitude. Make the necessary adjustments so that your attitude can be as positive as possible. Read Philippians 1:6.

_____

_____

_____

_____

_____

_____

Day 361

"DON'T ALLOW YOUR SITUATIONS AND CONDITIONS TO AFFECT YOUR ATTITUDE."

Points to Ponder

Recall a time when you went through a negative experience but God allowed you to overcome it. How did you manage the experience so that it wouldn't have a negative effect on your attitude?

_____

_____

_____

_____

_____

_____

Day 362

"WHEN YOU'RE ELEVATED, YOU NEED TO MAKE ADJUSTMENTS."

Points to Ponder

How committed are you to making the necessary adjustments for success when you are promoted?

_____

_____

_____

_____

_____

_____

Day 362

"EXTRAORDINARY PEOPLE LIVE BY HIGH STANDARDS."

Points to Ponder

Seek God today concerning the standards by which He wants you to live. Read Matthew 6:33.

_____

_____

_____

_____

_____

_____

Day 363

"EXPECT EXCELLENCE!"

Points to Ponder

Is excellence a part of your expectation? Write down your answer and explain why or why not.

_____

_____

_____

_____

_____

_____

Day 364

"AS DAVID WAS ELEVATED, HIS CIRCLE EVOLVED TO MATCH TWO THINGS: HIS SEASON AND HIS MATURITY."

Points to Ponder

As you experience elevation, follow David's example concerning the shaping of your circle. Your circle should match the season that you are in and the level of maturity that is necessary for you to maximize the season.

_____

_____

_____

_____

_____

_____

Day 365

"WE ARE ALL CAPABLE OF LIVING EXTRAORDINARY LIVES."

Points to Ponder

Read Matthew 19:26 and make the declaration that living an extraordinary IS possible!

_____

_____

_____

_____

_____

_____

Day 366

"EXTRAORDINARY PEOPLE MUST STEP UP!"

Points to Ponder

In what areas is God requiring or calling you to step up to challenges? Write down those areas and spend time praying about a strategy for stepping up.

_____

_____

_____

_____

_____

_____

Stay Connected!

BISHOP JOHN E. GUNS IS THE
AUTHOR OF

Seven Steps to Wholeness

AND EDITOR OF

The Soul of Manhood

FOR UPCOMING BOOK
RELEASES AND
ENGAGEMENTS, VISIT
WWW.BISHOPJOHNGUNS.ORG.

FOR INQUIRIES, CONTACT
THE **JEG** TEAM AT
FIRSTASST@SPMBCJAX.ORG
OR
904-768-7112.